PRAYER MATTERS

DISCOVERING THE JOYS OF GOD'S DESIGN
FOR A LIFE OF PRAYER

BY

REMCO BROMMET

ISBN: 9798481229355 - Paperback
Independently published

Cover & Interior design by Jennifer Brommet

Front Cover photo Jennifer Brommet
Back Cover Remco's headshot by Sophia Brommet

Contents

Introduction

"Prayer Matters" is a book for Bible-believing, born-again Christians who hunger for a deeper relationship with God and for more than occasional prayer. It can be read as a personal study, complete with practice exercises, or as a group study by using the questions for reflection and discussion. The title conveys a double meaning: that prayer matters, and that there are a number of matters to discuss concerning prayer.

As I begun the exciting task of writing this book, my mind frequently drifted to the condition of the world today. Perhaps yours does too as you begin reading.

We are experiencing turbulence of epic proportions: a global pandemic with travel bans and whole continents on lockdown, political and economic instability, increasing threats of armed conflict, quickly changing weather and climate patterns, and marked increases in crime and lawlessness.

As a result of the pandemic, pretty much the whole world went into an involuntary "Great Pause" that halted entertainment, sports, social gatherings, and commerce as we knew it. Churches had to close their doors to in-person services and ministries for a prolonged time, forcing worship and small groups to go online and ministry leaders to scramble for new ways of keeping their flocks connected. Many believers found themselves overwhelmed by it all, at a loss for how to respond, to understand what God was doing, or even maintain inner peace while facing so many challenges simultaneously.

Calls went out from faith leaders all over the world to see the pandemic in the light of God's exhortation to the people of Israel in 2nd Chronicles 7 - to respond to pestilences by humbling ourselves, seeking His face in prayer, and turning from our wicked ways. In other words: to use the pandemic and our period of voluntary and at times mandatory quarantine as an opportunity for reflection, repentance, and prayer.

Does the daily onslaught of unsettling news and the prospect of hard times for Christians unsettle you? I know it does me from time to time. But there is good news! Amid the turbulence, there is an ocean of love, comfort, strength, joy, peace, insight, and wisdom for those who want to walk with God.

That's why I am writing this book. Now, more than ever, God's people need to walk closely with Him. Despair over the world around us has a way of making us want to pray more. And that's exactly what God wants from us. He invites us to turn anger, helplessness and anxiety into prayer. He is there to help train us to do battle in prayer and develop prayer habits as natural and constant as breathing. He has given us the ability to learn to listen in prayer to His freeing, faith-building, peace-giving truths that give insight into our times, how to respond to what is happening, and help others.

The chapters are designed to help you understand and embrace the simple secrets that will move you from occasional prayer to a life of constant prayer. Unceasing prayer gives us access to the constant flow of His grace towards us. It unlocks the oceans of resources He desires to pour out into us.

The steadfastness of our faith and our ability to maintain joy and peace under pressure depend on us giving prayer the priority it deserves. God wants us to thrive in these times, not just hunker down and get by. Not only that, but He wants us to shine our light brightly, spread the aroma of Christ far and wide, and model peace and love to people who are feeling just as anxious and helpless as we are, but without hope. We can only do that if we are firmly connected to our heavenly Father through prayer. That is God's design for our lives, together as a community of faith and alone as

His individual children.

It is vital that we restore prayer to its proper place in our hearts, homes, and churches as a core discipline instead of an occasional safety net when things go wrong. We simply must make every effort to weave prayer into the fabric of our lives, not just on occasion but every day. It is the lifeblood of the relationship for which He created us and restored to us in Christ. It is what He desires from us when the world is shaking. And it is what we need in order to walk through the shaking with Him.

My encouragement to you is that prayer is not complicated. It does not involve a secret knowledge reserved for a spiritual elite. There are no hard-to-learn routines, no formulas to master, only Scriptural teaching to understand and examples to follow. Everything we need to learn is shown to us by the Son of God Himself, who has made communion with God simple and accessible, and modeled it as He walked among humanity.

Yet communion with our heavenly Father, who is invisible but always near, often goes quickly out the window when anxiety takes over and we get busy with problem-solving. We find it hard to be still when everything around us is moving at breakneck speed, and equally hard to listen to His still small voice when the world around us and unrest inside us scream at us from every direction.

I encourage you to read this book as a toolbox full of practical insights on God's design for a dynamic prayer life is. Receive it from one who has learned a thing or two, often the hard way, and is still learning. Let us agree to make prayer in its various forms a priority in our lives, a wellspring from which all our service, activities, ministries, and growth in wisdom, faith, love and understanding, flow.

While you learn to embrace prayer as a lifestyle, I believe with you that God will re-establish your life on a firmer foundation. He will give it new dimensions and greater depths. You will experience your very own spiritual awakening to all that God wants to be in, for you, and through you.

Thank you for reading!
Remco

Chapter 1
A Divine Connection

A man hung on a cross, his back bloodied by a Roman whip, his brow bleeding from a crown of thorns. His hands and feet had been nailed to a roughly hewn crossbar with large spikes, and his face was contorted in the unimaginable pain inflicted by one of the cruelest execution methods ever invented by human civilization. His crimes? Proclaiming the Kingdom of God, calling Himself the Promised Messiah, accusing the Jewish leadership of being hypocrites and whitewashed walls. A man of miracles and healing, a brilliant preacher who had fallen victim to betrayal, false accusations, humiliation, and torture. A sad ending to a brilliant ministry. It was the defeat of a new approach to faith in God, a new kingdom. Or so it seemed.

Jesus was God incarnate, who, out of unstoppable, unimaginable love for the rebellious human race He created, left divinity behind and *"emptied Himself to take on the form of a servant being born in the likeness of man, and being found in human form humbled Himself by becoming obedient to the point of death, even death of a cross"* (Philippians 2:8). What looked like defeat was God's ultimate victory over sin, death, and Satan's reign. Jesus' agony and death was followed by resurrection and ascension into glory. It was a pivotal point in human history that opened the door for sinful, rebellious humans, separated from God and worthy of eternal condemnation, to be forgiven, reconciled to God, redeemed, adopted as sons and daughters, and enter into a love relationship that starts on earth and goes on into all eternity. We call it "free grace," but for Jesus, it was expensive.

The backbone of that relationship is what we call prayer. God has chosen to pour Himself out into us through it, work through it, win victories over darkness through it. Prayer is the vehicle for just about everything in our relationship with God the Father.

To understand God's design for powerful and effective prayer, we have to pause a moment and talk about what prayer is and what it is not.

There are a lot of misconceptions floating around about prayer as a spiritual discipline. Many of those are rooted in our tendency to keep going back to the predictability of rituals, routines, and liturgy. We talk about "saying your prayers" and repeatedly recite predetermined form prayers in church services rather than using our own words. However, prayer was not intended to be a ritual or an empty form. But what is it, then?

Prayer Is A Gift From God

The Bible portrays prayer very differently. As we'll see in the following two chapters, prayer in the Bible leans more to the conversational – talking with God in not unlike the way people converse with each other. One of my favorite verses in Scripture is Exodus 33:11: *"Thus the LORD used to speak to Moses face to face, as a man speaks to his friend."*

As a man speaks to his friend. Unceasing friendship with our unseen Father in heaven. You might think, "that was Moses. He was a super saint and one of God's key leaders in the Scriptures. I am far from that." Don't sell yourself short! According to John 1:12, God has given to those who received Christ by faith the right to call themselves His children. The Father-child relationship already exists. Christ purchased it for us on the cross.

As a father to two daughters, I want an intimate relationship with them. I love them oh so dearly. I want to spend time with them and hear what is on their mind, and I want them to listen to me in return so they can learn from my life experience and wisdom. Why would that be different with God? We are reminded in the Scriptures over and over again that He loves us with such a great, supernatural love that, according to Paul, we have to have the help of the Holy Spirit in our inner being to understand the dimensions of that love (Ephesians 3:14-19).

And just as conversation and language are the gifts that make human relationships happen, prayer is the gift that makes our love relationship with God happen. He has all the time in the world, and His power is limitless. It never ceases to amaze me that He can listen to the prayers of, and reveal Himself to, millions of His children at the same time. And He knows all our needs, our thoughts, our motives, our joys and sorrows, our wounds and victories, our personality traits, our strengths, and weaknesses, better than we do. He knows everything about millions of people at the same time. That amazing miracle alone should make us want to run to Him in prayer!

Too Busy To Pray?

Yet, it seems that many of us are too busy to spend time with our heavenly Father. Surveys have shown that the majority of professing Christians spends at most five minutes a day in prayer. Maybe a hurried devotion in the morning, an activity-filled, fast-paced day during which most of us barely think about God, a blessing at dinner, and perhaps a prayer at night. Hardly the kind of intimate communication that makes for a good relationship.

In his book *The Ruthless Elimination Of Hurry*, American author John Mark Comer surmises that our faith's greatest enemy is not unbelief but busyness [1]. Constant distraction from the regular solitude and silence needed to commune with our unseen, unhurried God. Non-stop interaction with our electronic devices that programs our brains away from being able to be still and meditate on the abstract truths of Scripture. Overstuffed schedules that leave no time to rest, worship, connect with our families face-to-face, let alone give God our Father and Savior the firstfruits of our time and attention that He deserves.

When my now-grown children are too busy to keep in touch, I start missing them. I want to hear their voices again, see their faces, get hugs, and hear their news. And nothing gives me more grief than when their faces are buried in their cellphones and they seem to be too distracted to have a heart-to-heart conversation when we are together. If I feel that way as a human father, imagine how God must feel. After all, He paid the ultimate price so that we could experience His love into all eternity, instead of His wrath. He gave us the gift of unbroken access to His throne in prayer and awakened our spirits by giving us His Spirit so we can communicate with Him. He is eager to pour out all His love, His power, His wisdom, and His truth into us because He loves us. But He can't, because we cut ourselves off from Him.

Singer Larnelle Harris wrote and sang a song entitled *"I Miss My Time With You."* I remember hearing it on Christian radio for the first time. I felt instantly convicted. They sound like the words of the Father to me, His hurried, busy son. Especially this part:

"I miss my time with you, those moments together, I need to be with you each day; And it hurts Me when you say you're too busy; Busy trying to serve Me. But how can you serve Me when your spirit's empty? There's a longing in My heart, wanting more than just of you; It's true, I miss My time with you."[2]

We tend to busy ourselves with the tangible, the immediate, the tyranny of the urgent. As a result, God goes on the shelf, so to speak, for when we need Him as if He was pain medicine. We default to praying when we get in trouble or run into a problem we can't solve and pray out of need. But when things go well, we start coasting on our own power, and He goes back on the shelf.

Unceasing Communion

However, God intended for the gift of prayer to be a constant, unbroken, daily communion, a relationship driven by love. The apostle Paul wrote in Acts 17:28: *"in Him we live and move and have our being."* Another way of putting it is that we "abide in Him."

Jesus, His teaching always full of illustrations and parables, talked about this when He explained how the relationship between a human being and God as a heavenly Father was supposed to work. He likened it to that of a branch grafted into a vine (John 15:1-6). The sole responsibility of the branch is to hold on to the vine with all its might. As it does, the vine can intertwine with it and pour out its life-giving nutrients into the branch so it will produce fruit. Jesus wasn't just talking about plants. He was talking about us. He is the vine, and we are those branches. After we are reconciled to Him and have surrendered our life to Him, our sole responsibility is to hold on to the Father with all we've got so He can pour out His life into us. Jesus gives a simple bottom line: *"apart from me you can do nothing."* (vs. 5)

How do we do that? We hold on to Him through prayer. It is our divine connection to the Vine. We abide in Him through prayer. Our moving, living, and being in God happens through prayer. Without it, we stay spiritually asleep, and our life will be without growth or fruit. Jesus made that a dire warning in verse 6: *"If anyone does not abide in me (through prayer) he is thrown away like a branch and withers; and the branches are gathered, thrown into the fire, and burned."* A high price for prayerlessness.

A Two-way Street

A good relationship is a two-way street. You talk, and you listen. If you don't do both, the relationship fizzles. Likewise, prayer is not just talking to God but listening to Him. Says Andrew Murray: "Prayer is not monologue, but dialogue; God's voice is its most essential part. Listening to God's voice is the secret of the assurance that He will listen to mine." [3] If we only talk and neglect to listen, we cut ourselves off from the impartation of the most precious, life-giving, and empowering truths we can imagine. Now, who would want to do that?

Prayer is so much more than just talking to God. As you will discover in the chapters that follow, it is worship, adoration, surrender, making requests known, casting our anxieties on Him, listening, interacting with His Word, doing spiritual battle, and affirming His majesty. All that and more goes into fellowship with the Father, walking with God, all day, every day.

Make Room To Pray

Time to get practical. How do we get to that place of unbroken, unceasing communion with God, especially since our lives are so frantic and busy?

Understanding what a great gift prayer is and how important it is to God should motivate us to order our lives around communion with God. Here are a couple of suggestions that I have found helpful for my own prayer life.

1. *Make room in your heart* – The first step is to embrace by faith this amazing truth: God wants to reveal Himself to you as your Father and that you are His child, precious in His sight and dear to His heart. He wants you to delight in Him and to desire His presence. I didn't learn this myself until God yanked all my full-time ministry engagements out from under me for a year and a half. In that time, I learned that my relationship with Him had only been a business relationship It was all about ministry, and I involved God in little else on a personal level. I learned that God wanted me to be a son first and foremost and commune with Him as my Father. To learn to be, rather than do. And to realize that my doing should come out of my being rather than the other way around. Making room in your heart can be as simple as asking God to reveal Himself to you and to ignite in your heart a desire to be in His presence.

2. *Make room in your life* – That may be trickier. Maybe you are a busy mom whose children are up at the crack of dawn vying for your attention. Or you're dad locked in a career that demands every waking hour of your attention. But where there is a will, there is a way. Perhaps it involves training your children to give you an hour during a specific part of the day. Or to program prayer times into your work schedule. My suggestion: ask God to show you how to adjust your daily rhythm to give Him the firstfruits of your time. If "apart from me you can do nothing" is true, then He will help you make room in your life. I have found that at times I may not be able to have a quiet time at home, but I can pray, listen to worship music and the Bible on audio, and hear God speak to me while I drive. Other people use their daily exercise routine as a time to commune with God. You can go on a prayer walk or prayer run, for instance. Pray a quick blessing over people you encounter. Pray for people in distress as an ambulance or fire engine passes by on its way to an emergency. Pause and pray a quick prayer for help as you encounter a problem at work or at home. Our days are loaded with opportunities to commune with God when we look for them.

3. *Make room in your home* – It helps to have a designated place for prayer, a specific spot associated with the purpose of communion with God. It could be a porch, a study or reading room, even a closet – something made famous by the movie *The War Room*. It could be just a chair. Some people have found it nearly impossible to designate a place for prayer inside and prefer to go outdoors. Perhaps your car is your prayer closet, or a nearby park where you can be in nature and away from the hustle and bustle. And that is the point: to have a place away from noise and distraction so you can focus on the stillness in which God speaks, and you can sense

His presence. Jesus taught the disciples that they should go into their room to pray to the Father in secret and not do it publicly to be seen. The Greek word for room (tameion) can mean closet, storage room, or barn. The idea is to be alone with God, away from where all the action is. Jesus Himself exemplified that. He sought out gardens, mountains, and other nature spots away from the public eye to commune with His Father in heaven.

4. *Practice His presence* - Paul exhorts us in 1 Thessalonians 5:17 to *"pray without ceasing."* I have learned that it is possible to maintain a continuous sense of God's presence and be with Him in the moment, all day long, no matter what you are doing. Dr. J. Oswald Sanders, late General Director of the Overseas Missionary Fellowship, once said that one of the greatest secrets of effective prayer is the use of our discretionary time. According to studies, people spend at least 3 hours a day in total waiting for something or idling. Are you standing in line somewhere? Pray. Are you walking from one place to another? Pray. Are you stuck in traffic? Pray. Filling that idle time by seeking God will help you maintain a sense of abiding in Him – the notion that He is always there, always near. That sense of near-ness makes it a lot easier to pray in-depth because you don't have to overcome the feeling that God is far away. The phrase "practice His presence" comes from a book by Brother Lawrence entitled *Practicing the Presence of God.* [4] Brother Lawrence spent most of his life in a Carmelite monastery in Paris in the 1600s, where he learned to commune with God throughout the day - not just during the mandatory prayer services but also while performing menials tasks. It is a simple principle that goes a long way in making all forms of prayer powerful and effective. Another example of that is Concerts of Prayer founder and leader David Bryant. During meetings, he would suddenly

pause and address the Lord during the conversation, pulling him into our discussion as if He were physically sitting at the table with us. In David's experience of the abiding presence of God, He was.

After practicing His presence for a while, your daily walk with God begins to feel like you have a visible person with you, to whom you turn at a moment's notice for conversation. Far-fetched? God is real, He is omnipresent, and He has given us by our rebirth a spiritual antenna to pick up the signal of His presence. All it takes is practice, which is why it is called "practicing His presence."

The bottom line is that we have to be intentional about prayer because it is the backbone of our daily walk with God, both in the calm and in the storm. Our intentionality shows that our hearts desire Him and that He is uppermost in our thoughts and affections. Getting there involves fighting off distractions from within (our flesh, that wants to be gratified and entertained) and without (Satan, who fears and therefore hates prayer).

Nothing is sweeter, warmer, more peace-giving, and joy-sustaining than an unbroken sense of God's presence and a never-ending stream of truth, strength, guidance, provision, and protection that comes from being connected to God.

Prayer Practice

There is nothing like forging iron while it is hot. Now that you have read four steps toward creating a habit of prayer in your daily life, why not put them into practice right away?

1. *Examine your heart.* Do you believe that God truly loves you, delights in hearing your voice in prayer, and wants to speak to you? Look up some verses in Scripture that affirm that: John 3:16, Romans 8:38, 39, 1 John 5:13-15, John 15:1-11, John 16:13-15.

2. *Ask God to help you believe and listen.*

3. *Examine your schedule.* Can you designate a daily time set aside for prayer? It should be enough time to calm your busy mind and focus on the things of God. What do you need to adjust, and what arrangements do you need to make to protect that time?

4. *Examine your home.* Is there a place you can designate for prayer so that it becomes associated with that in your mind? What distractions do you need to remove from your

14

designated place? Can you place a Bible and a prayer journal there as the tools for fruitful, two-way communication with God? If there is no place in the house, is there some other spot conducive to communion with God?

5. *Examine your daily activities.* How much "idle time" do you have during your day that might provide opportunities to check in briefly with God through a prayer of thanks, a quick request, or even a momentary thought about His presence with you that keeps the unbroken connection going?

You have now set out to practice the presence of God by unceasing prayer. Keep it up! It takes at least twenty-one days to form a new habit. If there is a day that you can't make it happen, don't be discouraged. Show up again the next day and try again. I have found that God is way more patient with us than we are with ourselves. He honors your desire to commune with Him, and He will help you.

Questions for Reflection and Discussion

1. Have you had misconceptions about prayer?

    If so, what were they?

2. What obstacles against making room in your heart for God have you found while reading this chapter and doing the Prayer Practice?

3. In what ways is your daily schedule of activities hindering your efforts to give God the "firstfruits" of your time and attention?

Chapter 2
A Divine Design

When Jesus began his to teach about God's kingdom, the idea of a personal relationship with God through prayer was entirely foreign to the Jewish masses. Up to that point, direct communication with God had not been possible for anyone but a priest. The temple priests were the intermediaries between the people of Israel and God. So, the idea that an individual could simply talk to God without going through a priest was unfamiliar and possibly even objectionable. As the disciples spent their days with Jesus, He not only modeled communion with God to them, but He laid out a divine design, a blueprint for prayer.

The Blueprint from the Savior

He laid out that blueprint in response to a simple request from them: *"Lord, teach us to pray."* (Luke 11:1). We see from the opening line of the verse that Jesus had been praying "in a certain place," so we can safely assume that His disciples were there with Him. They had heard Him talk about prayer but had no clue how it was supposed to work.

We know the divine design Jesus unveiled as "The Lord's Prayer," and we find it along with varying accounts of His teaching in Matthew 6:5-15 and Luke 11:1-13.

Before we unpack its meaning, let me make it clear that the phrase "The Lord's Prayer" is itself not in the original Greek text. Chapters, verses, and headings were added later by Bible translators to make it easier to read. In the case of Jesus' teaching on prayer, this is unfortunate because it tricks the reader into thinking that Jesus gave us a particular wording for prayer that we are supposed to repeat. And indeed, for many, that is what

The Lord's Prayer has become. We have put it on plaques and in church services' liturgies as a prayer that is to be recited verbatim as a ritual as if it has some magical power. I have sat in Sunday services where we collectively prayed it aloud and found my mind wandering to lunch after the service while I mumbled the words to this profound pattern for prayer. Methinks I was probably not the only one. Conversations with fellow believers from various church backgrounds have shown me that for quite a few, the mindless mumbling of the Lord's Prayer gives a sense of reassurance that God has heard us since we prayed in His own words. For many who consider themselves Christians, daily communion with God is not a reality. So they substitute conversation with God with ritualistic prayer in church, forgetting that mindless rituals were the very thing that upset God about Judaism and that Jesus railed against in many of His sermons. While reciting the Lord's Prayer is in itself not a bad thing and can be quite meaningful and comforting, mindless repetition is not what Jesus intended.

In all fairness, the opening lines of the Luke 11 account, *"When you pray, say..."* (verse 2), would suggest that Jesus gave us words to repeat as a divinely approved prayer. But the context of His teaching on prayer indicates otherwise. Matthew 6 vs. 9 bears that out: *"Pray then like this:"* (ESV). The NIV puts it: *"This, then, is how you should pray."* From the word "how," it becomes clear that Jesus wasn't giving His disciples a rote prayer to recite, but rather a pattern, a blueprint, a divine design for prayer.

A builder has to study the blueprints of an architect to build a house correctly. Similarly, we have to learn how our faith was designed by its Architect (1 Peter 2:15) to know how He wants us to commune with Him and order our lives around walking with Him through prayer. So, let us look at these blueprints together.

Reverence

Our Father in Heaven. We begin with the correct posture

in prayer. I'm not talking about physical posture like kneeling or standing, though those are not unimportant as an expression of our inward posture. That inward posture – the posture of our heart, if you will – is what Jesus is talking about here.

He instructs His disciples to address God as "Father." The Greek word in Matthew 6:9 here is "Pater," which is the same as the Aramaic word "Abba," sometimes used for God (Romans 8:15). Both are terms that combine familiarity with reverence. Familiarity is the sense that we have a personal relationship with Him. Reverence is the sense that He is our Creator and therefore a higher Being.

That is further accentuated by the qualifying words that follow. God is not just any Father, but our Father in heaven, a reverent acknowledgment of Isaiah 55: 8, 9 – *"For my thoughts are not your thoughts, neither are your ways my ways, declares the Lord. For as the heavens are higher than the earth, so are my ways higher than your ways and my thoughts than your thoughts."*

So the phrase "in heaven" is a reference to the level of God's ways and thoughts rather than His actual location.

Some popular Bible expositors have suggested that to address Him with "Abba" means to call Him "Daddy." That may be emotionally appealing, but according to quite a few Bible scholars, dead wrong! Abba is a transliteration from the Aramaic term "Ba" or "Va," which was often used to address teachers of the law and members of the Sanhedrin. It means the same as the Greek word "Pater," also a term of respect.

The point is that we come to God with reverent hearts, knowing that He is far superior to us, that He is our Creator and Sustainer, and we are mere created beings. Yet we come with the understanding that He is not distant or indifferent as had become the case in the Judaic view of that day, but that we have a personal, intimate relationship with Him. He comes to us as a loving, gracious, and empowering God, with wisdom, knowledge, truth, and ways of doing things that we do not have and sorely need.

Worship

Hallowed be Your Name. Once the posture of our hearts is right, we begin with worship. Jesus teaches His disciples to say, "hallowed be your name." What does "hallowed" even mean?

The Greek word here is "hagiasthētō," which means both "to make holy" and "to venerate." So why not just say: "We adore You" or words to that effect?

Because through Jesus' teaching, God wants us to see Him as our perfect Father, not just with superior thoughts and ways, but also one who is holy and therefore worthy of reverence. He is holy because there is not even a speck of evil, sin, infirmity, or imperfection in Him. There is nobody in all the universe like that. He alone is worthy of our adoration and our worship. He alone deserves to be uppermost in our thoughts and affections.

Beginning our prayers with worship is significant because it has a way of aligning our hearts with Him and building our faith. Our lives are already full of worship more than we realize. We worship all kinds of things. I'm not just talking about figures of clay and wood or stars or saints here. I'm thinking more about all the things that we give more time and attention to than we do to God. Stuff like entertainment, sports, creature comforts, money, possessions – things that feed the desires of the body and the mind (Ephesians 2:3). Things that, at least on the surface, fulfill some emotional need and give us significance in our own eyes and, we hope, in the eyes of others.

Starting our prayers with worship gets our eyes off those things and gets us thinking about God. His perfections, His love, His grace, His faithfulness, His mercy, His wisdom, His power, His glory. It's pretty much doing what this well-known hymn by British missionary Helen Lemmel encourages us to do:

"Turn your eyes upon Jesus
Look full in His wonderful face
And the things of earth will grow strangely dim
In the light of His glory and grace." [1]

I love the last two lines of that hymn because they spell out precisely what worship does: the more we look to Him, the more insignificant all the other stuff we tend to care about becomes.

Worship not only lifts our hearts to God the Father and helps us see Him in the proper perspective to ourselves, but it also builds our faith. The more we see God's greatness, the easier it becomes to trust Him.

Surrender

Your kingdom come, Your will be done on earth as it is in heaven. Blueprints for a physical building assume that the structure you build will go vertical and that each layer forms the foundation for another. Jesus' blueprints for powerful and effective prayer work that way as well. Our correct view of God evokes worship from our hearts, which in turn helps us see His divinity in all its grandeur and builds our faith. On top of that, it softens our hearts for the next step: surrender.

My Practical Theology professor in Bible College used to say: *"In the Lord's Prayer, we pray for missions before we ask for our daily bread."* I have reflected on that a lot over the years and have come to see that the phrase "your kingdom come, your will be done on earth as it is in heaven" refers to much more than just global missions.

It brings us to a place of voluntary and glad surrender to God based on what we have seen of Him in our worship. Acknowledging that His ways and thoughts are higher than mine and gazing upon His greatness makes it easier to surrender to God's will and reign. I know it to be wise, loving, and benevolent (cf. Jeremiah 29:11).

Not just that, but He created me to be dependent on Him, and dependence involves a willing surrender to the power of another.

Surrender also puts us in the frame of mind to want to pray what He desires: To seek His glory and not our own. To want the advance of His purposes and His kingdom and not our own agendas. We must get there before we start asking for things because of our sin-soaked human nature. Sin in us wants to put our desires first, wants to be our own God, and determine our future. If we don't address that by intentionally surrendering to God, we are tempted to ask for things that we want and that we think we need. Not only is that a form of unbelief because we secretly do not trust God to know what we need without us spelling it out for Him, but it is also an underhanded way of trying to get what we want out of life rather than letting God determine that for us.

Last but not least, surrender prepares our hearts to receive from Him what we need, rather than what we want. Even if it looks different than what we expect. We trust that Father knows best. We accept that He will meet our needs according to His will and wisdom, for His glory, and for the advance of His reign on earth. Surrender is an expression of trust. Let's say you have a piece of jewelry that broke. You take it to a reputable jeweler to get fixed because you are unable to do that yourself. You surrender your prized possession to the repairman in full assurance that he knows what he is doing and that he will fix the problem. You don't hang around, hover over him and start giving him advice on how you want him to fix it. The result of your trusting surrender is that you'll receive it back repaired and probably looking better than before. You have no idea how he fixed it, but his workmanship enhances your respect for him and your trust in his abilities. You'll want to go back for more repairs. You sing his praises to others, and his reputation grows. Likewise, our surrender to God to meet our requests His way and in alignment with His will ultimately will result in greater glory for Him as you trust Him more and more when He answers your prayers in His wisdom and you share your experiences with others.

Supplication

Give Us This Day Our Daily Bread. Once we have God in His proper place, worshipped Him, and surrendered to His will and reign, we are in the right frame of mind to ask Him to meet our needs, as well as the needs of others. This part of the prayer blueprint is called supplication. It comes from the Latin verb "supplicare," which means "to plead humbly." *The Oxford Dictionary* defines it as "the action of asking or begging for something earnestly or humbly." [2] Think of it as putting into practice Paul's exhortation in Philippians 4:6: *"Do not be anxious for anything, but in everything by prayer and supplication with thanksgiving let your requests be made known to God."* Since Jesus tells us to address God as "our" Father, and He phrases His instruction as asking for "our bread," we have to think of the asking as inclusive – i.e., not just on behalf of ourselves but of others as well. Pleading with God on behalf of others is what is commonly called "intercession."

What might confuse us about this part of the blueprint is the phrase "our daily bread." What is Jesus talking about here? Bakery goods? Groceries in general? Money? Is He referring to primarily physical needs like food and shelter?

Our daily bread encompasses much more than the concrete, three-dimensional word pictures Jesus often uses to represent abstract spiritual ideas. Those word pictures were often rooted in Old Testament symbolism familiar to His disciples and the crowds who came to listen to. "Bread" is mentioned 492 times in the Bible. It stands for God's provision for physical nourishment (cf. Exodus 16), spiritual nourishment, life and salvation (cf. John 6:35), God's Word (cf. Deuteronomy 8:3, Matthew 4:4), and fellowship with Christ (cf. Luke 14:15).

When Jesus invites us to ask God for our daily bread, He invites us to ask Him to meet our physical, emotional, and spiritual needs. In short, everything. You can fill in your own blanks – a lot of blanks.

"Give us this day our daily bread" is a statement of complete dependence on Him. In it, we express the truth that Jesus taught us in John 15:5 about life with Him as God designed it: "...apart from me you can do nothing." To pray this way for ourselves and others is the antithesis to life according to our sinful nature, which says, "I can do it by myself."

True Identity Ministries, which my wife Jennifer founded in 2008, operates by the motto "Everything by Prayer." It is an expression of that very truth from John 15:5. Not that we can't do anything ourselves or shouldn't do anything at all. We intentionally make ourselves dependent on Him in everything because that is what God had intended for mankind before sin entered the human race. We have adopted it as a motto for how we want to live as well. I have discovered quickly that "everything by prayer" is harder than it sounds because of our constant bent toward independence and pride. Independence wants us to have things our way, and pride wants to crow about our achievements in life. Since "supplicare" means to plead *humbly*, and we are praying from a place of surrender, there is no place for independence or pride. Or the thought that I can fix this issue myself. The struggle between our independence and living in dependence on God is real and life-long. I am still learning to involve God in every aspect of our daily lives and the lives of others.

Not to say that we should not work for our food or sit around and do nothing. Jesus said: *"Apart from Me,"* you can do nothing. Our doing comes out of our being in a relationship with the Father, Who guides us according to His will, instructs us according to His truth, empowers us, provides for us, and protects us. All that is wrapped up in the meaning of "give us our daily bread." We ask for daily life-giving, nourishing, empowering, fellowship-enhancing, truth-teaching provision for ourselves and for others. We have none of that in ourselves. All of it comes from our Father in heaven.

Confession and Forgiveness

Forgive Us Our Debts As We Have Forgiven Our Debtors. This part of God's design for prayer seems a little confusing at first. Two questions immediately arise: Should I keep asking for forgiveness of my sins (debts) when Jesus paid the penalty for my sin on the cross and canceled my sin debt (cf. Colossians 2:14)? And what has forgiving others to do with prayer?

The answer to the first question is yes. To be sure, Jesus died on the cross for our sins, and as a result, there is no condemnation for those who are in Him (cf. Romans 8:1), and nothing can separate us from His love (Romans 8:38,39). As a result, we are saved from the coming wrath and judgment of God. However, we still struggle with sin (cf. Romans 7:23). We still have a bent towards independence and self-glorification. "I did it my way" is not only a famous song but the anthem of everyman which continues to offend God (which we don't want to do), and leads us afoul of His purposes for us.

Therefore, every time the Holy Spirit causes a pang in our conscience about something we have said, done, or even thought, we have to confess it and ask God to forgive us of that sin. It is worth taking a look at two verses in 1 John 1: *"If we say we have no sin, we deceive ourselves, and the truth is not in us. If we confess our sins, he is faithful and just to forgive our sins and cleanse us from all unrighteousness."* (vs. 8,9). I think this means that every time the Holy Spirit makes us aware of a sin we have committed through a pang in our conscience, God wants us to confess it. Then He can forgive and cleanse us and thus restore our relationship with Him along with our ability to pray to Him unhindered. We can't pray and ask God for things when our relationship with Him is broken, even in the smallest of ways. Think for a moment about the relationship between a parent and a child. A child is guaranteed the love of its parents as long as they are alive. But when he or she breaks the rules that have been set, the ordinarily loving relationship is temporarily broken. Not the love in the parent's heart, just the day-to-day interaction. Not until the child fesses up, asks for, and receives forgiveness is normalcy restored.

Confessing our sins as we become aware of them, and asking God for forgiveness, is an essential part of our daily prayers. It ensures a clean heart, a clear conscience, and an unbroken relationship with the Father.

What about forgiving others? Jesus considers this of such great importance that He adds some additional teaching about it in the verses immediately following His discourse on prayer:

"For if you forgive others their trespasses, your heavenly Father will forgive you, but if you do not forgive others their trespasses, neither will your heavenly Father forgive your trespasses." (Matthew 6:14,15)

Ouch! Forgiving others is crucially important to keep our relationship with the Father in the right standing. Because God forgave us all our trespasses, we are to forgive others theirs. Jesus further stresses that through the parable of the unmerciful servant in Matthew 18. The forgiveness of our sins came at the expense of Christ's agony on the cross and should therefore be considered by us as very precious and costly. By forgiving others, we are paying it forward. By not forgiving others, we show ourselves to be undeserving of God's forgiveness. A high price to pay for keeping a grudge!

It is interesting to note that Jesus uses two different words in His teaching: He tells us in vs. 12 to ask God to forgive our debts (Greek opheilēmata) and tells us to forgive others their *trespasses*

(Greek paraptōmata). The first word denotes more severe transgressions, and the second word is used for minor slip-ups and errors. Because God forgave us all our major transgression (and minor ones!) toward Him, He expects us to be quick to forgive others, even their minor slip-ups toward us. The greatness of God's forgiveness toward us is the motivator for our forgiveness toward others.

So forgiving others is an important aspect of our daily prayer habits. It is a good practice to make a shortlist in your head every night before going to bed and to state your forgiveness of each person you got angry at or frustrated with that day -from the guy who cut you off in traffic to the co-worker who said something insensitive, and everyone in between. Forgive them from the heart as God forgave you.

Spiritual Warfare

And Lead Us Not Into Temptation, But Deliver Us From Evil. As soon as someone surrenders his life to Christ, he is drafted into the battle between God and Satan. The outcome of that battle is already set. But there is plenty of fighting in between.

Renowned author and pastor Dr. John Piper often employed a short rhyme in his teaching about prayer:

"You cannot know what prayer is for until you know that life is war." [3]

It is not an intercom or bell to summon a maid or butler to fluff up your pillows and cater to your every need.

The apostle Paul describes that battle like this: *" For we do not wrestle against flesh and blood, but against the rulers, against the authorities, against the cosmic powers over this present darkness, against the spiritual forces of evil in the heavenly places."* (Ephesians 6:12)

It may be a bit perplexing that Jesus instructs us to pray for God to not lead us into temptation. We get the 'deliver us from evil" part as our cry for God to protect us from Satan's attacks, but does God lead us into temptation? In a short article for Desiring God Ministries, John Piper addresses it like this:

"So God does not do the tempting—he does not put evil desires in our hearts (for he can have no evil desires in his heart)—but he does bring us into the presence of many tests and temptations. '"A man's steps are from the Lord"' (Proverbs 20:24)

In fact, every step we take is a step into the presence of temptation. There is no moment of your life that is not a moment of temptation—a moment when unbelief and disobedience is not a possibility. The Lord's prayer does not teach us to pray against that kind of sovereign guidance. What it teaches us to pray is that the temptation does not take us in. Don't lead me into temptation. Deliver me from this evil that is set before me." [4]

Perhaps the verse makes more sense if we understand that the Greek word (peirasmon) used here has multiple meanings. It can mean a test of one's faith, character, or virtue. It can mean exposure to adversity or evil, and it can mean the lure of something that appeals to our sinful desires. According to the book of James, chapter 1 verse 13-15, temptation does not come from God, but from either Satan stirring our sinful nature. And so we pray that God will not allow evil to overcome us but rather deliver us from it.

We live on a planet occupied by Satan's forces of evil that hate us. For that reason our daily prayer habits should include vigilance and seeking God's involvement anything that tempts us to be discouraged, doubtful, deceived, or distracted from our walk with Him. I make it a daily practice now to put on the armor of God Paul describes in Ephesians 6:13-17. I paraphrase it, turning the Roman war attire's mechanical components and what they symbolize into a prayer pledge for my walk that day. It goes something like this:

"Father, today I pledge, with the help of your grace and the

power of the Holy Spirit who lives in me, to walk in your truth, with my heart protected by the righteousness given to me as a gift purchased by the blood of Christ on the cross whereby I stand free from any accusation or condemnation. I am ready to share the gospel of peace at all times, in word and deed. I set my mind on the things that are above in accordance with my salvation which has brought me into your kingdom. I go forth holding up the shield of faith against all that the enemy throws at me today, knowing that he has already been defeated and has no claim on me. And I wield the sword of the Spirit by letting your Word dwell in me richly."

Substitute your own wording or even pray for each part of the armor of God literally. The goal is the same: that we start our days with God, in God, serving God, and well aware that we are at war.

Faith Affirmation

For Yours Is The Kingdom And The Power And The Glory Forever. Every sung and recited version of The Lord's Prayer has this beautiful affirmation of faith, followed by a resounding "Amen." But in the Bible, you'll only find it in the footnotes with the remark "some manuscripts add." It means that most manuscripts of Matthew's gospel used for translation do not have those words.

However, I think they are significant and, in my humble opinion, beautifully round out God's blueprint for prayer.

We began with worship and adoration of God's Name. We end with proclaiming that all our prayers are based on our belief that His kingdom, His power, and His glory will be forever. I can't think of a greater affirmation of our love and admiration for God and our faith in His greatness. Such proclamations of His glory as affirmations of our faith are significant because, like worship, they build our faith. Paul says of Abraham in Romans 4:20, 21: *"No unbelief made him waver concerning the promise of God, but he grew in his faith as he gave glory to God, fully convinced that He was able to do what He had promised."*

See? He grew in his faith as he gave God glory, which led to his unwavering conviction that God would keep his promise. Likewise, all our worship, surrendering, asking, pleading, interceding, and spiritual battle are rooted in the unshakeable conviction that God's kingdom, power, and glory will last forever. Regularly declaring that in prayer is an act of worship and an act of unwavering faith.

Our prayers should contain an element of preaching to our own souls. As we worship and speak out our love and admiration for the attributes of God, we take our eyes off the daunting challenges we are praying about and see only Him. Like Peter, we can walk on the wind-swept waves then. We cast our eyes on Him, and our soul is rapt with the assurance that He indeed will answer our prayers and fulfill His promises – for the sake of His kingdom, power, and glory!

The Divine Design Is No Drudgery

Designs or blueprints are never meant to be rigid. They are supposed to leave room for changes, for creativity. They are guidelines to follow, not an ironclad grid from which no one is to depart. That is the same with Jesus' teaching on prayer. In giving us "The Lord's Prayer," He provided us with specific elements for powerful and effective prayer. But He never intended for it to be a rigid pattern that we should repeat the same way day after day for our prayers to be pleasing to God.

In the conversational piece of our relationship with God, Jesus invites us to include all these elements regularly, but not necessarily in the same way and in the same order. Rejoice in the great privilege that we may start every prayer we pray with these incredible words: "Our Father, Who is in heaven." Those words incline His ear to you and stir your heart to express itself in the most authentic way possible in worship, surrender, supplication, spiritual battle, and affirmation of faith.

Prayer Practice

Now that we know that the Lord's Prayer is more of a template for prayer than an actual prayer to be repeated, let's work with it. Take a journal and put each line of the Lord's prayer in your own words as your own prayer.

Example:

Our Father Who is in heaven: My heavenly Father, my Father who sees and hears me from heaven, etc.

Hallowed be your Name:

Your kingdom come:

Your will be done on earth as it is in heaven:

Give us this day our daily bread:

And forgive us our debts:

As we also have forgiven our debtors:

And lead us not into temptation:

But deliver us from evil:

For yours is the kingdom and the power and the glory, forever. Amen:

Now you have a beautiful prayer, according to God's design, written out to express your heart to God. Pray it back to Him. Keep it in your journal to refer back to from time to time as you grow in your prayer life. Over time, praying this way – spontaneously, but within the divine design elements, will become second nature.

Questions For Reflection And Discussion

1. Read The Lord's Prayer (Matthew 6:9-13) out loud, together or alone. Which phrases appeals to you the most, and why?

2. Forgiving others as God forgave us is an important "hidden" element of a fruitful prayer life. Why?

3. The final part of The Lord's Prayer is an affirmation of our faith that all the power and the glory in the universe belongs to God. If you were to write your own affirmation of faith, what would it be?

Chapter 3
The Prayer Life of
Bible Heroes

Prayer is more caught than taught. In other words, you learn the most from watching it in action in people's lives. Such was the case with Jesus' disciples. They asked Jesus to teach them after watching Him pray and being inspired by what they saw. Likewise, it is helpful for us to look at a few heroes from Bible history whose lives illustrated the different elements of God's divine design for prayer. What makes their examples encouraging is that, except for Jesus Himself, they were flawed people. And yet, they lived close to God. Even Jesus makes prayer relatable since He walked on earth as a plain human experiencing the same struggles and temptations as we do, yet making Himself entirely dependent on God the Father through prayer.

Reverent Intimacy: Moses' Friendship With God

In chapter one, I mentioned that Exodus 33:11 is one of my favorite verses in the Bible because it describes the prayer relationship between God and Moses as a friendship: *"Thus the Lord used to speak to Moses face to face, as a man speaks with his friend."* It is preceded by this detail, recorded in verse 8 and 9: *"Whenever Moses went out to the tent* (that is the Tent of Meeting, also known as the Tabernacle), *all the people would rise up, and each would stand at his tent door, and watch Moses until he had gone into the tent. When Moses entered the tent, the pillar of cloud would descend and stand at the entrance of the tent, and the Lord would speak with Moses."* What a beautiful picture of the relationship between a human being and his heavenly Father! This daily conversation between friends comes after a lengthy session on Mount Sinai where Moses received the Ten Commandments, the law, and the instructions for the Tabernacle, worship, and priesthood. He got so close to the presence of God that when he returned to the camp, his face shone so brightly that he had to cover it because people couldn't look at him without being blinded.

This description of Moses' relationship with God tells me what God desires for all of us in our prayer life: that we spend time with Him, listen to Him, and bring our requests and concerns before Him with the reverence of a created being for the Creator and the intimacy of a close friendship. The Tent of Meeting symbolizes our prayer closet, or, for that matter, any place and time that we pause and pray. The pillar of cloud is God's manifest presence that is in us and around us at all times, day and night, and becomes visible to our spiritual eyes by faith.

Moses' fallibility should encourage us that such intimacy with God is not beyond our reach. After his initial but murderous bravado as a prince of Egypt, he had to flee to the desert and work as a shepherd for forty years (Exodus 2:11,12). By the time he was ready to receive his calling, he had to be persuaded patiently by God speaking to him from a burning bush to rescue his people and lead them out of Egypt. During the exodus, he disobeyed God's instructions (Numbers 20-1-13) and was denied entry to the Promised Land as a result. While leading the tribes through the desert, he lost his temper (cf. Exodus 32:19,20) and had to be talked into getting help with judging the people (Exodus 18:13-24). Yet God spoke with him every day as a friend. What an amazing reality. There is hope for all of us! By His grace, in His love, He lets us call Him Father, and He offers us His friendship.

That is an important notion to hold on to because it represents the spirit in which Jesus gave us the divine design for prayer. The combination of worship, reverence, surrender, expressing needs, confession of sin, praying for protection, and affirming the greatness of God express emotions similar to the ones you may have for a close friend or a beloved father. You think the world of him (worship), and you trust him (surrender). You are not afraid to seek his help and protection (supplication and spiritual battle). You seek his forgiveness when you have wronged him (confession and forgiveness), and you will constantly affirm how great and precious he is (the affirmation of your faith and love). The only difference is that they are expressed to God with humble reverence and not with a casual kind of familiarity.

Worship: Mary's Song

The gospel of Luke is the only gospel that details the events leading up to the birth of Jesus Christ. Those details include a beautiful song of praise by his mother Mary, which later became known as one of the first Christian hymns – *The Magnificat* [1]

According to Luke 1:36, Mary and Elizabeth were relatives, most likely cousins. When Mary heard from the same angel who announced she would give birth to the Savior that Elizabeth was also pregnant with a son in her old age, she rushed to her house and spent three months with her. As Mary first burst through the door of her cousin's house, Elizabeth's unborn son leaped in her womb. She was filled with the Holy Spirit and proclaimed a blessing over Mary for being "the mother of her Lord." (Luke 1:39-45).

Mary responded with this song, recorded in Luke 1:46-55: *"My soul magnifies the Lord, and my spirit rejoices in God my Savior,*
For he has looked on the humble estate of his servant.
For behold, from now on all generations will call me blessed;
for he who is mighty has done great things for me, and holy is his name.
And his mercy is for those who fear him from generation to generation.
He has shown strength with his arm;

he has scattered the proud in the thoughts of their hearts;
he has brought down the mighty from their thrones and exalted
those of humble estate;
he has filled the hungry with good things, and the rich he has sent
away empty.
He has helped his servant Israel, in remembrance of his mercy,
as he spoke to our fathers, to Abraham, and to his offspring
forever."

Her worship is rooted in her obedience and unreserved surrender to God's plan to carry and give birth to the Savior. It displays a deep recognition of the holiness, mercy, strength, providence, and the promises of God to Israel throughout history and, on this day, to her.

It is not uncommon to see prophets, leaders, preachers, and other key figures in the Bible recite the entire history of God's mighty deeds before speaking about what He is doing, or is about to do. You will find a similar approach to David's worship in the Psalms. Doesn't that get a little long-winded, you ask?

Perhaps, but God is never in a hurry, and neither should worship be. I have found that one of the most meaningful forms of worship is unhurried basking in His presence while meditating elaborately on the great things He has done. That gives our soul much greater joy in Him and builds our faith much more solidly than some hasty and vague words of praise or thanksgiving lobbed toward heaven. I have been guilty of doing that myself, in a phase of life when I was always in a hurry, so I know the difference and have come to value unhurried, Christ-exalting, faith-building adoration.

But why the constant recital of God's mighty deeds in the past? Couldn't I just focus on what He means to me today? Sure you can, and that is not wrong by any means. But periodically remembering His mighty deeds throughout history gives a greater grandeur to what He is doing in your life and the lives of those around you today. There is something awe-inspiring about realizing that the same God who did such astonishing things throughout history knows you and is listening to your worship and prayers with the heart of a Father.

Mary's Magnificat is by no means a prescription for worship that we must follow each time we burst into praise. But remembering God's grace toward us, His holiness, strength, protection, providence, and promises today and throughout all of history is a helpful enrichment of worship, both private and public.

Surrender: Jesus in Gethsemane

When Jesus taught us to pray, "your kingdom come, your will be done on earth as it is in heaven," before praying for anything else, He introduced a principle that He lived Himself. Our Lord sought the Father alone in quiet places before making any major ministry decisions like selecting His core team of disciples. He said so in John 5:19. *"So Jesus said to them, "Truly, truly, I say to you, the Son can do nothing of his own accord, but only what he sees the Father doing. For whatever the Father does, that the Son does likewise."* He lived, ministered, and taught out of total identification with the Father's will.

That complete identification with God's will and kingdom purposes led to an inner struggle to the point of sweating blood in the Garden of Gethsemane the night before His crucifixion. His closest disciples were unaware of what was about to unfold, even though Jesus had told them many times over what would happen to Him and why. The account in Matthew 26:26-46 says that they succumbed to sleep while Jesus went off by Himself to seek the Father once more. He was sorrowful and troubled (vs.37). Three times He fell on His face in agony and prayed, *"My Father, if it be possible, let this cup pass from me; nevertheless, not as I will, but as you will."* (vs. 39). The Luke account adds that an angel of heaven ministered to Him and that while He prayed in agony,

"His sweat became drops of blood falling to the ground." (Luke 22:43,44).

For a moment, the Son of Man became a regular human being who knew what was about to happen and was terrified. Anyone who has seen a Roman execution would be. But He knew it was His mission, and there was no escape. It had to be completed for all humanity. The temptation to avoid pain and suffering and to preserve His own life was real. But the knowledge of what was at stake won out. His struggle is what brought the writer to the Hebrews to say about Christ the High Priest in Chapter 4:15 – *"For we do not have a high priest who is unable to sympathize with our weaknesses, but one who in every respect has been tempted as we are, yet without sin."*

This vivid depiction of Jesus' surrender to the will of His Father contains some important lessons for the way He wants us to pray. We must first understand that the heart of our sinful nature is the desire to be God. We go to great lengths to fulfill the desires of our mind and body, to preserve our interests and lives, to get what we think we are entitled to, and to determine the outcome of our lives. Even when we are in prayer, we can be tempted to forget our surrender and repentance when we first gave our lives to Christ and instead project our selfish desires unto God.

To earnestly pray "your will be done" requires a death to self. Jesus' struggle pointed to that when He faced the actual death of His body on the cross. When we surrender to His will, we face the death of our sinful selves – purposely considering our desires of no value. It can sometimes become a downright fight when our interests and passions and those of the Father collide, especially when we pray for ourselves or people near and dear to us. But we have to overcome our self-will and surrender if we ask God for things according to His will, especially since that is one of the prerequisites for Him hearing our prayers (1 John 5:14). God's desire for our prayer life is that we arrive at the same acquiescence Jesus did in the Garden: *"Not my will, but yours be done."* When we do, we will learn quickly that the Father always knows what is best for us, whether we understand that or not.

I had a rather painful and public lesson of surrender to God's will when I attempted to organize a large prayer rally on the National Day of Prayer. It is a day set aside for prayer by presidential proclamation and falls on the first Thursday of May. It was to be held outside the State Capitol of Minnesota, in the Northern US. We had always held smaller gatherings there at noon, but I wanted to go big, so I proposed a mass rally in the evening. Despite usually iffy weather in early May, we always had a ray of sunshine and no rain for an hour or so during that noon hour while we prayed with state senators and representatives. We rented sound equipment, hundreds of chairs, a stage, and lighting for the evening rally. We promoted it heavily and received an encouraging response. I was full of excited anticipation of a powerful rally. Surely God would bless this! But, on the night of the blessed event, it poured. Torrential rain. All afternoon and all evening. Rain so hard, the equipment could not even be set up. I wound up having to put in an emergency call to the main local Christian radio station to announce that the event was canceled. We lost thousands of dollars in rental fees.

No rally. No prayer. In my shortsighted arrogance, I was furious with God. As I sat in my car seething while the rain kept thundering on the roof, one of the program leaders, a well-respected pastor, spotted me and ran over. As he hastily dove out of the storm and into the passenger seat next to me, he immediately read my face and simply said: *"Brother, God is sovereign. If He wants to rain on His parade, that is His right and His decision, and we cannot and should not question it."* Then he hopped out and left. As my anger at feeling let down by God in the work I thought I was doing for Him slowly subsided, thoughts began to pop up in my mind that I knew came from the still small voice of the Holy

Spirit. Patient, loving, but stern thoughts. *"Whose will was this, Remco? Yours or mine? And for whose glory was this? Yours or mine? Did you ask me first if this is what I wanted, or did you just go ahead, expecting me to bless your plans for a big rally?"* I had to seek His forgiveness for my lack of surrender and learned an important lesson. No prayer should be prayed or ministry undertaken without a clear understanding of, and submission to, His will and purposes. Even in Jesus' life, surrender to His Father's will was at the center of everything.

Supplication: The Prayer Life of David

When you read through the book of Psalms and look at the 75 or so David wrote you see a broad range of prayers: worship, adoration, thanksgiving, desperate pleas, repentance, and urgent cries for provision and protection. They were rooted in a life lived entirely outside the comfort zone. Suddenly yanked away from his safe, simple life as a shepherd, he wound up face-to-face with the meanest, tallest, baddest, and most fearsome fighter of the Philistine army and defeated him with a sling and a few stones. He spent the next few years on the run from the jealousy of Saul, who he was to succeed as king, hiding in caves and dodging constant attempts on his life. David fought battles for the borders of his kingdom during most of his reign. He went through a deep valley of sin and repentance when he lusted after the wife of one of his most trusted soldiers and had him killed in battle so he could have her. The child this affair produced got sick and died. Then his older, deeply beloved son Absalom turned against him and was killed, causing him unspeakable grief. And despite all these things, God Himself said of David: *"I have found in David the son of Jesse a man after my heart, who will do all my will."* (1 Samuel 13:14, Acts 13:22). Why would God say that? I think it is because David learned to lean on God for all of his needs, spiritual, emotional, and physical, with humility, desperation, and reverence. Most of his prayers of supplication were for spiritual sustenance, the lifting of his spirits, or deliverance from his enemies. Here is a small taste:

"Open my eyes, that I may behold wondrous things out of your law." (Psalm 119:18)

"Let your steadfast love comfort me according to your promise to your servant. Let mercy come to me, that I may live; for your law is my delight." (Psalm 119:76,77)

"Make haste o Lord, to deliver me! O Lord make haste to help me! Let them be put to shame and confusion who seek my life!" (Psalm 70:1,2)

His song of thanksgiving to God for His covenant as recorded in 1st Chronicles 16 describes David's heart and explains why God loved Him: *"Seek the Lord and his strength; seek his presence continually!"* (vs. 11)

It is in that constant seeking of God's presence that reverent, humble prayer and intercession – asking God to meet my needs and those of others – becomes a life-long habit. And since Jesus instructs us to ask God for our daily bread, we know that daily dependence on God for all our needs through prayer is His desire for us. David recognized it as mercy – undeserved and unmerited, and as a privilege granted solely by the love of God and not by how lovable or how deserving we are. So should we!

Intercession: Abraham's Prayer for Sodom

"So the men turned from there and went toward Sodom, but Abraham still stood before the LORD. Then Abraham drew near and said, "Will you indeed sweep away the righteous with the wicked? Suppose there are fifty righteous within the city. Will you then sweep away the place and not spare it for the fifty righteous who are in it? Far be it from you to do such a thing, to put the righteous to death with the wicked, so that the righteous fare as the wicked! Far be that from you! Shall not the Judge of all the earth do what is just?" And the LORD said, "If I find at Sodom fifty

*righteous in the city, I will spare the whole place for their sake."
Abraham answered and said, "Behold, I have undertaken to speak
to the Lord, I who am but dust and ashes. Suppose five of the fifty
righteous are lacking. Will you destroy the whole city for lack of
five?" And he said, "I will not destroy it if I find forty-five there."
Again he spoke to him and said, "Suppose forty are found there."
He answered, "For the sake of forty I will not do it." Then he said,
"Oh let not the Lord be angry, and I will speak. Suppose thirty are
found there." He answered, "I will not do it, if I find thirty there."
He said, "Behold, I have undertaken to speak to the Lord. Suppose
twenty are found there." He answered, "For the sake of twenty I
will not destroy it." Then he said, "Oh let not the Lord be angry,
and I will speak again but this once. Suppose ten are found there."
He answered, "For the sake of ten I will not destroy it." And the
LORD went his way, when he had finished speaking to Abraham,
and Abraham returned to his place."* (Genesis 18:22-23)

Abraham had an intimate relationship with God. His plea on
behalf of the wicked city of Sodom came on the heels of God's
promise that all nations would be blessed through his offspring.
Shortly after that, God promised a son in his old age. Two things
jump out from Abraham's prayer of intercession: his humility and
genuine brokenheartedness over the city's impending destruction
and the collateral loss of life. He is in his nineties now, and these
are the fruit of God's work on his character.

Abraham's prayer is intercession at its most authentic:
representing a city lost in sin before the throne of grace to plead
for mercy. I believe this is a foreshadowing of one of the most
important roles of the risen Christ. Paul tells us in Romans 8:34:

*"Who is to condemn? Christ Jesus is the one who died – more
than that, who was raised – who is at the right hand of God, who
is indeed interceding for us."*

We are as lost in sin as the people of Sodom were, and often
unawares. Despite the righteousness we received as a gift from

God in response to our repentance, Jesus intercedes for us daily because we continually veer back toward sin. The one difference is that Sodom could not be spared, but we, who have been made righteous by the Savior's blood once for all, receive daily grace, mercy, and love from the Father as a result of Christ's death, resurrection and intercession.

We can learn from Abraham that intercession is both deeply humble and unselfishly compassionate. It is humble and unpresumptuous because we approach God on behalf of others solely based on Jesus' atonement for our sins. God does not hear our prayers because we have merit or deserve to be heard. Christ purchased our ability to approach God with His death on the cross. Intercession is unselfishly compassionate in that we do not seek our agenda for the person we represent in our prayers, but only God's plans for their wellbeing. We want His will to be done in them, not ours. We come out of godly love, not out of a selfish desire to get involved in their problems or seek credit for bringing about God's intervention.

The third lesson from this account is that God does not always grant our requests on behalf of others. In Abraham's case, God's answer was not to spare the city because he could not even find ten righteous people in it. God knew that already, but Abraham did not. I think God allowed him to express his compassion in prayer because He delighted in that part of Abraham's spiritual growth.

Perhaps this has happened to you as well. It certainly has to me. I fervently prayed for decades that my parents and older siblings would come to Christ. Yet, both my parents and two of my older brothers died without knowing Him. I inquired of God about that, and He assured me that in answer to my prayers, they were given the opportunity to repent and receive Christ but refused.

Moreover, praying for them this way helped me see them through God's eyes, feel the compassion He wanted me to have for them despite unhealthy family dynamics, and express that to Him in prayer. God always answers, but His answer may not necessarily be what you hope for or expect. It might even be a resounding "no." And through our prayers for others, He changes us.

The bottom line is this: we should always intercede for others with humility and compassion, knowing that God has decreed to work mightily through the prayers of His people. At the same time, we must surrender our expectations of an answer to His sovereign will and His superior wisdom.

Confession of sin and forgiveness of others: Ezra and Stephen

During the tribe of Judah's exile in Babylon, a remnant had returned to Jerusalem under Zerubbabel, who had found favor with king Cyrus, to rebuild the temple. Once it was finished and dedicated, Ezra, a scribe and descendant from Aaron, went up to Jerusalem to start teaching the law of Moses to the people living there. After several generations in exile, they had to relearn how to worship God, rid themselves of sin, and adapt to living under God's law instead of Babylon's laws. We pick up the story in Ezra 10:1 with a poignant scene:

"While Ezra prayed and made confession, weeping and casting himself before the house of God, a very great assembly of men, women, and children, gathered to him out of Israel, for the people wept bitterly."

This is a powerful illustration of the prayer "forgive us our debts" from the prayer Jesus taught us – a prayer that should recur in our communion with God regularly.

Ezra knew that even though they were God's chosen people and He had shown them miraculous favor by leading them out of slavery once more to rebuild the temple, worship and teaching of the law needed to begin with a confession of specific sin.. Ezra wept and cast himself down before the temple while he prayed.

He was soon joined by a very great assembly of people who also wept bitterly. That could only have come from a deep conviction of collective sin by the Holy Spirit

When we get sloppy about sin – a little dishonesty, a little gossip, a little lust, a little neglect of our prayers and meditation of the word – it starts to come between God and us and opens the door for Satan to regain his hold on us. It is essential for us to end our days by spending some time with the Father and asking Him to show us if we have grieved or neglected Him in any way. When He convicts us in our conscience, we confess in specific terms and seek His forgiveness and cleansing. Heartfelt confession expresses our desire to please the Father in every way and keeps our communion with Him unbroken.

Ezra's confession, and that of many other reformers in the Old Testament, most likely included godly sorrow over the entire nation's sins, forebears included. I have found that often, as I pray for my fellow believers or our country, I feel the weight of collective sin as a nation that turned its back on God and as a church that has become too comfortable. At times, it is just a weight that casts me down. At other times, it feels like anger, and occasionally I feel deep sorrow. I am not alone in this. I have heard of many fellow intercessors who feel a burden to confess collective sin as the Holy Spirit leads.

Then there is the other half of that line in the Lord's Prayer: "...as we forgive our debtors." Remember that asking God for forgiveness for our sins does not work unless we forgive those who sinned against us? Such was the case with Stephen. He was the first deacon to serve in the fledgling community of faith in Jerusalem, a man "full of faith and of the Holy Spirit" (Acts 6:5). He did great signs and wonders among the people. That, along with the wisdom and power of his preaching, did not sit well with local synagogue leaders, so they brought him before the Sanhedrin, where he preached his most powerful sermon yet.

His words enraged the Jewish leaders, so they dragged him out of the city and stoned him, making him the first martyr for the Christian faith. He could have resisted, pled his case, breathed talk of vengeance, or cursed his executioners, but he did none of these things. Acts 7:60 described what he did instead:

"And falling on his knees he cried out with a loud voice, 'Lord do not hold this sin against them.' And when he had said this, he fell asleep." That was very much the spirit of Christ in him. Jesus had cried out similar words while dying on the cross, *"Father forgive them, for they know not what they do."* (Luke23:34).

His example embodies the power of forgiveness. In the same way that the Father forgives me for treating him unjustly by grieving Him, so I am to forgive others who grieve me by treating me unjustly. From the guy that cuts me off in traffic to the burglar who steals my stuff all the way up to being wrongly imprisoned, mistreated, or put to death. Forgiveness is not an option. Paying God's forgiveness forward by forgiving others, whether we think they deserve it or not, is key to maintaining a good relationship with the Father and to unhindered prayer.

Spiritual warfare: Hezekiah's Battle and the Believers' Prayer for Boldness

Hezekiah was one of the good kings of the southern kingdom of Judah. According to 2 Chronicles 29:2, he *"did what was right in the eyes of the Lord, according to all that David his father had done."* That uprightness and loyalty were severely tested when king Sennacherib of Assyria invaded Judah and laid siege to Jerusalem. He belittled the God of Judah because of his many victories over God's people and tried to persuade Hezekiah to give up Jerusalem or face horrible consequences. While the story is only mentioned briefly in 2nd Chronicles 32, it is told much more elaborately in Isaiah 36 and 37, most likely because it took place during Isaiah's ministry in Judah. It is one of the most encouraging stories of deliverance in the entire Bible. It also qualifies as a spiritual battle because there was more at stake than the freedom and lives of Jerusalem's inhabitants. Sennacherib blasphemed God and questioned Hezekiah's faith in a letter he sent him. Hezekiah's response was to take that letter to the temple and spread it out before the Lord. Then he cried out for deliverance in a prayer that could not have been longer than thirty seconds, calling God's attention to the words of Sennacherib and turning the battle over to Him. Why? Merely to save people's lives and guarantee their freedom and prosperity? Hezekiah doesn't ask for that. He says:

"O Lord our God, save us from his hand, that all the kingdoms of the earth may know that you alone are the Lord." (Isaiah 37:20).

God's glory is at stake, more so than the wellbeing of the people.

God's response to Hezekiah's 30-second prayer is spectacular. He gives him a promise through Isaiah that starts with the words *"because you have prayed to me concerning Sennacherib king of Assyria"* (Isaiah 37:21). Because you turned the battle over to me, Hezekiah, because you sought my glory before your own, I will act on your behalf and destroy Sennacherib. That very night an angel of the Lord came and silently struck down 185,000 Assyrians (Isaiah 37:36). When the people of Jerusalem woke up the following day, they saw nothing but dead bodies and empty tents. Sennacherib and a handful of survivors had slunk back to Nineveh. A short time later, he was murdered by his own two sons.

In spiritual warfare, we turn the battle over to the Lord. Hezekiah's prayer was basically the same as what Jesus taught us to pray: deliver us from evil. For our sake? No, for more than that. For the glory of God, for His is the kingdom, the power, and the glory forever.

We find another powerful example of a power encounter between good and evil in Acts 4, when the "believers," those who had come to Christ during the early days of the church, prayed for boldness in the face of their first persecution. Peter and John had been seized and warned to stop preaching Christ under threat of severe punishment. When they returned to their friends, they all lifted their voices together to God in prayer. They did not ask for safety or even protection from threats of persecution. Instead, they saw the threats for what they were: an attack on the gospel that Jesus commanded them to preach (Matthew 28:19), and therefore an attack on God's kingdom. Like Hezekiah, they called God's attention to the threats of the chief priests and end their prayer with a simple but profound request:

"And now Lord, look upon their threats and grant to our servants to continue to speak your word with all boldness, while you stretch out your hand to heal, and signs and wonders are performed through the name of your holy servant Jesus." (Acts 4:29,30).

God's response is instantaneous:

"And when they had prayed, the place in which they were gathered together was shaken, and they were all filled with the Holy Spirit and continued to speak the word of God with boldness." (4:31)

An attempt had been made to snuff out the spread of the gospel and put an end to the Great Commission. The salvation of humankind was at stake. The realization of God's kingdom on earth was at stake. In the minds of these men who were completely sold out to Jesus, that threat far outweighed their safety. They, too, turned the battle over to God for the glory of His name.

That is the point of spiritual warfare. Our aim is not the solution to a problem we face or the end of a threat to our safety and comfort, but rather a thwarting of Satan's attempt to derail our mission and oppose God's kingdom. Whenever that happens, we place ourselves under God's protective cover by turning the battle over to Him for the sake of His glory.

Faith Affirmation: The Apostle Paul

We cannot discuss examples of Bible heroes' prayer lives without considering the prayers of the Apostle Paul. As Saul, he had overseen Stephen's stoning and set out on a mission to stomp out this new Jesus sect called the Way - until he met the One whose followers he was persecuting face-to-face on the road to Damascus. The encounter left him blinded, humbled, awestruck, and profoundly in love with Christ, his Savior and Lord. He called himself "the least of the apostles" (1 Corinthians 15:9) because he had persecuted the church. As a matter of fact, that is what his new name, Paul (derived from the Latin word "Paulus"), means: "small" or "humble." Out of this deep sense of humility, he wasted no opportunity to magnify Christ as he staked his life on His grace by faith.

That worshipful affirmation of faith often shines through in his prayers for the believers in the churches he planted. Prayers like this one, in Ephesians 3:14-19:

"For this reason I bow my knees before the Father, from whom every family in heaven and on earth is named, that according to the riches of his glory he may grant you to be strengthened with power through his Spirit in your inner being, so that Christ may dwell in your hearts through faith—that you, being rooted and grounded in love, may have strength to comprehend with all the saints what is the breadth and length and height and depth, and to know the love of Christ that surpasses knowledge, that you may be filled with all the fullness of God."

Talk about praying for daily spiritual bread! It is followed by this worshipful affirmation of faith in verse 20-21:

"Now to him who is able to do far more abundantly than all that we ask or think, according to the power at work within us, to him be glory in the church and in Christ Jesus throughout all generations, forever and ever. Amen."

His words of exaltation are very much along the lines of the doxology in The Lord's Prayer: *"For yours is the kingdom, and the power, and the glory forever, Amen!"*

He prays a similar prayer for the Colossian believers:

"And so, from the day we heard, we have not ceased to pray for you, asking that you may be filled with the knowledge of his will in all spiritual wisdom and understanding, so as to walk in a manner worthy of the Lord, fully pleasing to him: bearing fruit in every good work and increasing in the knowledge of God; being strengthened with all power, according to his glorious might, for all endurance and patience with joy; giving thanks to the Father, who has qualified you to share in the inheritance of the saints in light." (Colossians 1:9-12).

He concludes his prayer with this affirmation:

"He has delivered us from the domain of darkness and transferred us to the kingdom of his beloved Son, in whom we have redemption, the forgiveness of sins."

Pray these intercessory prayers and the affirmations of faith they contain over the lives of fellow believers and your own life as well. They are in part a proclamation to our own soul of God's greatness and in part an expression of worship.

We've looked at a smattering of examples from the prayer lives of Bible heroes. There are many more. What is encouraging about them is that these were people like us. They made mistakes, they sinned, they struggled with weaknesses, they often managed to grieve God despite their devotion, and yet look what God was able to do with them and through them. The apostle James even reminds us of that:

"Elijah was a man with a nature like ours, and he prayed fervently that it might not rain, and for three years and six months it did not rain on the earth. Then he prayed again, and heaven gave rain, and the earth bore its fruit." (James 5:17-18).

He and the accounts of all these real people in the Bible cheer us on to not give up praying and make it the main priority of our daily lives with a God Who wants to be our all in all.

Prayer Practice

Let's take a page from the Apostle Paul's book on prayer to practice following the example of a Bible hero in his prayer life:

1. Write in your journal a short list of people near and dear to you who you want to see grow in their walk with Christ or, for that matter, enter into a relationship with Him for the first time.

2. Look up Paul's prayer for the Ephesians in Chapter 3: 14-19. Substitute the name for each person you have written down for the word "you."

3. As an affirmation of your faith that God will answer your prayer, pray Paul's doxology in verses 20 and 21.

Questions For Reflection And Discussion

1. Which of the Bible heroes whose prayer life we examined appeal(s) to you the most, and why?

2. We have looked at some very specific prayers that some of the Bible heroes prayed. Which one(s) would you want to regularly pray for yourself, and perhaps others?

3. Many of the people in the Bible who were friends with God were deeply flawed, which should give us hope! What would friendship with God look like for you?

52

Questions For Reflection And Discussion

1. Which of the Bible heroes whose prayer life we examined appeal(s) to you the most, and why?

2. We have looked at some very specific prayers that some of the Bible heroes prayed. Which one(s) would you want to regularly pray for yourself, and perhaps others?

3. Many of the people in the Bible who were friends with God were deeply flawed, which should give us hope! What would friendship with God look like for you?

Chapter 4
He Helps Us In
Our Weakness

When Jesus taught his disciples about prayer, He laid out a divine design, a blueprint, for how we should pray, which we examined in chapter two. We surmised that The Lord's Prayer is not a prayer just to be memorized and recited. Rather, it is a collection of different elements that should go into a vibrant prayer life.

Then, we read what the Apostle Paul says in Romans 8:26. *"Likewise, the Spirit helps us in our weakness. For we do not know what we ought to pray for as we ought, but the Spirit Himself intercedes for us with groanings too deep for words."*

A couple of translations, like the NASB, use the word "how" – we do not know *how* to pray as we should.

Why, if the Savior Himself told us how to pray, does Paul say we do *not* know and need the help of the Holy Spirit?

The answer lies in the accuracy of the translation. In verse 26, the Greek verbiage (to ti proseuxōmetha) means literally "what things to pray for." That is a gamechanger. Jesus gave us God's design for what our prayer life should consist of. However, that still leaves us wondering what things we should pray for so that our prayers can safely be on Jesus' behalf (in His name) and according to God's will. Both are stressed by Jesus (John 16:23) as well as John (1 John 5:14) as important qualifiers for our prayers to be heard.

Our knowledge on this side of heaven is very limited, so the Holy Spirit comes in to help us in our weakness. Romans 8:26 suggests that He prays both *in* us and *through us*. That is one of the most freeing and faith-bolstering verses in the Bible concerning prayer. I am not left to my own devices to figure out what I should pray or doubt whether what I pray is according to God's will and therefore acceptable to Him. But how exactly does this work? How does the Holy Spirit help us when we pray?

It happens in two ways: The Holy Spirit tells us what to pray for people and situations, and He Himself prays for us. The first involves learning to listen to Him, the second understanding what it means that we are the temple of the Holy Spirit.

The Freeing Secret of Listening Prayer

During my earlier years in ministry as a prayer mobilizer for revival and spiritual awakening, I often admired people with a call to intercession on their life. They could spend hours a day in prayer as if time stood still, while I struggled to stay focused for thirty minutes. A bit jealous of such powerful and effective prayer, I asked the Lord to make me more of an intercessor. I forgot I had prayed that until we moved from the West Coast of the US to the East Coast. All ministry ceased for eighteen months! I soon discovered that God wanted to show me that I had limited my relationship with Him to a business partnership. His desire for me was to have a deeper personal intimacy with Him. The secret? I learned to listen to the Holy Spirit about what I should pray.

Rather than bombarding God every morning with a list of requests for myself and others, I learned to begin with the simple question: *"Father, what is it that you want to say to me today?"* I took a step of faith that the God who answers prayer would show me what Scripture to read, what insight and application I was supposed to receive. He did, with clear and deep thoughts that were far too brilliant and deep to have come from my own superficial mind. Perhaps for the first time in my life, I learned to recognize the Father's voice speaking to me by the Holy Spirit. No dreams, no visions, no flashes of light or burning bushes. It was just a still small voice that presented itself as persistent thoughts that I recognized as different from my own. I felt like I was learning to put into practice Paul's exhortation preceding Romans 8:26, namely Romans 8:1-11 – walking in the Spirit and setting my mind on the things of the Spirit because the Spirit dwells in me.

That changed the way I prayed as well. The more I learned to listen to the Holy Spirit, the more insecure I grew about the accuracy of my prayers. Were they really according to God's will, or were they just what seemed logical to me? Was I just relaying my ideas of what God should do for me and others? Or was I genuinely praying according to the affirmation, "your will be done on earth as it is in heaven?" So, I decided to begin my prayers with the confession: *"Father in my weakness I do not know what I ought to pray for"* and the request: *"What is it that you want me to pray? Holy Spirit, please bring to mind the prayers God wants me to pray back to Him that are according to His will and not my own."*

It changed my prayers dramatically. Generalities like "be with," "bless," "help" began to disappear. My prayers became much more specific and faith-filled based on the knowledge that the Holy Spirit was helping me know what to pray.

It is a growth process. It starts with the step of faith that the Holy Spirit indwells you and wants to reveal God's truth, God's perspective, and God's insights to you. Not just understanding of spiritual things, but also practical directions in what to pray. I've found it helpful to meditate on the passages in the gospel of John where Jesus lays out the work of the Holy Spirit:

"But the Helper, the Holy Spirit, whom the Father will send in my name, He will teach you all things and bring to remembrance all that I have said to you." (John 14:26)

"When the Spirit of truth comes, He will guide you into all the truth, for he will not speak on His own authority, but whatever He hears He will speak, and He will declare to you the things that

55

are to come. He will glorify Me, for He will take what is Mine and declare it to you. All that the Father has is Mine; therefore I said that He will take what is Mine and declare it to you." (John 16:13-15).

Voice Recognition

How do you recognize the Holy Spirit's voice once you have made time and room in your heart and home to seek stillness and start listening to Him? It happens through practice. Jesus tells the disciples in John 10:4,5: *"When he has brought out all his own, he goes before them, and the sheep follow him, for they know his voice. A stranger they will not follow, but they will flee from him, for they do not know the voice of strangers."* Recognizing a specific voice over others comes by focusing on that voice and tuning out all others. Just like a bank teller learns to recognize counterfeit money by studying the feel and look of real money, we learn to recognize strange voices the more we get to know the voice of God.

That practice begins with knowing the Scriptures. They are the infallible, authoritative, God-breathed revelation of God. Paul says in Ephesians 6:17 that the Spirit is the Word of God. The majority of what He reveals to us comes through His Word. That is why it is *"living and active, sharper than any two-edged sword, piercing to the division of soul and of spirit, of joints and of marrow, and discerning the thoughts and intentions of the heart."* (Hebrews 4:12). Even when He speaks to us directly with His still small voice, He will never contradict Scripture.

Satan tries to use the Word too. He did so with Jesus while trying to tempt Him in the desert. However, he will take verses out of context and twist their meaning to lead you astray. How will you know the difference between truth and lie if you do not know the Word? Therefore, knowing your Bible is an essential, lifelong practice that will help you recognize His voice and follow

Him with confidence. Listening Prayer and the Word are never far apart! And the more we practice hearing His voice through the Word and in conjunction with the Word, the easier it becomes to let the Holy Spirit pray through you by bringing thoughts into your mind to pray back to God - prayer thoughts that are clearly recognizable as coming from Him and not from your own logic or Satan's lies. In fact, the more you know the Word, the more you wind up praying Scripture back to God on behalf of yourself or others.

Practice makes perfect. It implies failure and error, especially in the beginning. But God is on your side. At times He will be more persistent in what He says as my mind wanders off and starts listening to other voices. And every time you do wander off, once you realize you have been listening to the wrong voice and come back, another lesson is learned, and His voice becomes a little clearer the next time you get confused.

No Slacking!

One of the keys to successful voice recognition is not slacking off. Anyone who does sports or plays a musical instrument has learned that lesson. If you slack off and take a break for a couple of days, your muscle memory goes, and you have to start all over again. For instance, when I have been going to the gym consistently and then stop going for a week, I wind up having to set all the counterweights to lower settings the first time I go back. The same goes for music. Concert pianist Yuja Wang said in an interview that changing the finger setting or even the emotional mood of a piano piece requires an additional six hours of practice for the changes to become muscle memory in her hands and fingers.

Our partnership with the Holy Spirit in prayer is no different. If recognizing His voice and listening to Him requires practice, then the practice must be consistent. And since practicing voice recognition only happens in fellowship with Him, our time alone in prayer and meditation on the Word must be frequent and consistent.

Simple enough. Prayer and meditation on the Word are the two most foundational spiritual habits a Christian ought to have. Yet sadly, for many of us, they are the most neglected ones. We would rather sit in church listening to a sermon or attending a potluck than spending an hour or so a day in prayer. Frankly, I am no exception to this. It took a long, long time for me to reach consistency. I have had Attention Deficit Hyperactivity Disorder (ADHD) for most of my life, so consistency was a struggle with anything, let alone communing with a God Who I could not see or meditating on a big book without pictures. I learned from experience how easy it is to slack off, skip your quiet time by telling yourself you'll do it tomorrow, and then not to get back to it for a week. Or two. Before you know it, depression and anxiety return, lies that you had renounced and replaced with God's truths begin to crop back up, and God feels really far away. Recognizing the voice of the Spirit and getting back to a place where you are aware of His presence and His voice speaking to your mind is now suddenly much harder.

My first turning point in this pattern came as a young student at a British Bible College, long before ADHD was even recognized. I felt convicted over my lack of discipline by watching many of my fellow students scattered about the student lounge and other common areas every morning with their heads bowed over their Bibles in prayer. I tried and tried but just could not get myself going. One day Dr. J. Oswald Sanders, author and former General Director of the Overseas Missionary Fellowship, came to our College for a few days of speaking and ministry. I decided to take my discipline dilemma to him. Walking into his room, I felt about as big as an ant. I was in the presence of someone who radiated the godliness that comes from spending much time in the company of the Lord. After I explained my difficulty in overcoming a lack of discipline, he looked at me and said: *"Your problem is not discipline. It is desire. You get up for breakfast every morning, don't you?"*

"Uhm, yes.

"Why?"

"Because I'm hungry."

"So, you can get yourself out of bed with great consistency because you are hungry for food. But you are not hungry for spiritual nourishment. Your problem is not that you lack discipline but that you lack the desire to be in the presence of God. And God wants you to come to Him out of desire for Him, not out of mere obligation or self-discipline."

That was a painful but important turning point in my life. I realized that I did not desire God for who He was, primarily just for what He could do for me, so I only prayed when I needed Him. Even though I had been a Christian for some time, and I was studying for full-time ministry, the concept of fellowship with Him was unfamiliar. Yet, at the same time, it was strangely inviting. After my conversation with Dr. Sanders, I confessed my lack of desire for Him and asked the Lord to ignite a yearning for His presence more than for what He could do for me

As a result, my consistency in spending time with God began to improve significantly because it was motivated by a desire for Him in good times and bad, rather than just a need for Him. That is not to say I did not struggle. I had to ask for that desire to be reignited many times over as I got too busy and distracted. Doing is easier for me than being. Action is more attractive than silence. But it eventually improved when I established a morning routine that begins with a quiet time in a designated place before doing anything else. I learned to get ready for that routine before going to bed the night before by praying that God would awaken me with His thoughts in my mind and a fresh desire in my heart to be in His Presence. And God, Who is on our side and wants to meet with us, has always answered that prayer.

Your Pen Can Help You See

Early on in my spiritual walk, a wise mentor taught me the importance of journaling as part of my quiet time. Journaling, of course, can mean different things. Some people use a journal to write down significant occurrences each day or important information like ideas, recipes, quotes, and other items worth remembering. Others journal activity progress and health data during exercise and diet programs. I know quite a few Christians who use a prayer journal to put their prayers in writing and keep a list of who and what they pray for. And journaling through adversity and suffering is highly recommended by therapists as a way to express and process thoughts and emotions.

The journaling I have in mind is part of listening to the Holy Spirit. As He gives you insights into particular passages of Scriptures you are meditating on, it is important to write them down. The Lord told Habakkuk: *"Write the vision, make it plain on tablets, so he may run who reads it."* (Habakkuk 2:2). The implication was that He would write a revelation down for others to read. This is a good exhortation for us as well. Writing down insight into the meaning of a Scripture passage helps you remember it. Filling a whole journal with insights enables you to track your spiritual progress.

Another reason for journaling is perhaps not as obvious. I have heard it said that a pen can help you see. When you write down a thought or an insight, it makes room in your head for another. I put that to the test for myself, and sure enough – as I began to meditate on a particular passage of Scripture after asking the Holy Spirit what He wanted to say to me through it, I wrote down insights that popped up in my head. They were way too brilliant to have come from me. But here is the kicker: as soon as I had written down one, another would pop up, almost as if they were linked together as a train of thought – a divine train of thought. The process of putting one thought in writing made room for another, then another, and another. In other words: writing helped me see more.

Writing also helps with focus and organization. I found that when I just sit and try to think without writing anything down, the insights pop out of my mind as quickly as they pop in, as my distracted, hyperactive mind quickly wanders off to other things. Perhaps you cannot identify, but I need my pen and my journal to keep my train of thoughts on track.

And then there is the importance of remembrance. The Holy Spirit gives us insights into the Word of God, perspectives on life's situations and relationships from God's truth, as well as insights for intercessory prayer so that we will remember and use them. They become part of the spiritual knowledge base in our minds. The very act of writing them down engraves them in your memory, and even if amid the busy distractions of your day you still forget, at least you have written them down as a reference.

I now have a big stack of journals in all shapes and sizes dating back some 35 years. I am a wee bit jealous of my wife, whose journal pages are neatly arrayed and written in beautiful cursive. Mine are mostly written in a chicken scratch that is legible only to me. Sometimes I use diagrams and extra notes in the margin. And I do include prayer assignments, important events, and even writing or speaking ideas because they are often interwoven. Some entries are only a page long. Others take up multiple pages. A handwriting analyst might think that they are the expression of a furtive mind that thinks on the fly and struggles to stay organized. But at least it is there for me to reread or refer back to. There are occasional gaps, and I certainly do not journal every day. Still, I can say that keeping a journal has been essential for my spiritual growth as my main method for receiving and remembering insights from the

Holy Spirit.

The Holy Spirit Prays In Us

There is another way in which the Holy Spirit helps us in our weakness. Not only does He let us know what to pray, but according to Romans 8:26 He prays for us as well: *"...but the Spirit Himself intercedes for us with groanings too deep for words."*

How does that work? Oswald Chambers describes it best in *My Utmost For His Highest*:

"We realize that we are energized by the Holy Spirit for prayer; and we know what it is to pray in accordance with the Holy Spirit; but we don't often realize that the Holy Spirit Himself prays prayers in us which we cannot utter ourselves. When we are born again of God and are indwelt by the Spirit of God, he expresses for us the unutterable. 'He', the Holy Spirit in you, 'makes intercession for the saints according to the will of God' (Romans 8:27). And God searches your heart, not to know what your conscious prayers are, but to find out what the prayer of the Holy Spirit is. The Spirit of God uses the nature of the believer as a temple in which to offer His prayers of intercession." [1]

What an amazing reality! Whether you are aware of it or not, the Holy Spirit lives in you when you are born again. Your whole being is a temple in which He prays prayers for you that you yourself cannot utter. They are too deep for human words or thoughts. And the Father searches your heart to listen to what the Holy Spirit prays for you. All because our prayers as human beings are not enough in and of themselves. We need deeper prayer and more powerful advocacy to see us through our journey on this earth to our destination in heaven. I have sometimes wondered what the Holy Spirit prays for me. But since His prayers are too deep for words, they are also too deep for my understanding. I just have to accept in faith that He prays for me constantly.

It is a relief to know that whenever I have a shred of doubt that my prayers measure up to God's will, I may remind myself that the Holy Spirit prays in me because God understands and accepts that my own logic is not sufficient to pray effectively. Moreover, knowing that His Spirit is simultaneously praying in and for millions of fellow believers worldwide builds my faith in the might of my heavenly Father.

The apostle Peter reminds us that *"His divine power has granted to us all things that pertain to life and godliness."* (2 Peter 1:3). Those things include the Holy Spirit's indwelling to gives us insight for prayer in our conscious mind and to pray for us at a level too deep for us to understand. The reality of the prayer life of the Holy Spirit in us is both sobering and satisfying.

Sobering because it takes every excuse not to pray away from us. Satisfying, because we may know that He takes our prayers to the level they need to go to pray truly according to the will of God, and we don't have to try to do that in our own strength.

Prayer Practice

Buy a journal if you don't already have one and try incorporating this as a regular aspect of your devotional life and as a way to record insights God gives you for prayer.

To help you get start learning to listen to the still small voice of the Holy Spirit, consider following these simple steps:

1. Set aside a time to meet with God in the place you designated for prayer as part of the Prayer Practice in Chapter 1.

2. Remove any distractions from you: smartphone, computer, TV screen, etc.

3. Ask God one straightforward question: *"Father, what do you want to say to me today?"* Be silent, listen for passages of Scripture that He might want you to look at to pop into your head, or a word or phrase He wants you to think about.

4. Record any insights that look like revelations to you in your journal as they come—no need to be organized. Just write the date, any Scripture references, and what comes to mind.

5. If you start feeling a particular burden to pray about something for yourself or others, begin by asking: *"Father, what do you want me to pray?"* Listen for what pops into your mind, accept by faith that this is the Holy Spirit, and pray it back to the Lord.

Some mornings you are not going to get it together. At times you may feel confused about whether or not the Holy Spirit is actually the one speaking to you. Don't worry. Tell yourself you'll be back tomorrow to try again and accept that by practice, your recognition of the Holy Spirit's voice will get better because God is on your side, and He wants you to know His voice.

Questions For Reflection And Discussion

1. What are some of the fears you have about listening to God? What specific action steps could you take to overcome them?

2. This chapter highlights that knowing the Scriptures is one of the keys to recognizing God's voice. What have you found difficult about knowing and understanding the Word of God? What are some specific steps you could take to overcome those difficulties?

3. Are you struggling with discipline or motivation? How could you break through those struggles, alone or together with others?

Chapter 5
The Delight and Duty of Unceasing Prayer

My nightstand sports a wooden plaque my wife gave me for Christmas. It has the inscription *"Pray without ceasing,"* from 1 Thessalonians 5:17. Those words are the first thing I see through my blurry eyes when I wake up in the morning – a daily reminder of the exhortation Paul often gave to the believers in the churches he planted. He told his brothers and sisters in Rome to *"be constant in prayer"* (Romans 12:12), the Ephesian faithful to pray *"at all times in the Spirit"* (Ephesians 6:18), and the church in Colossae to *"continue steadfastly in prayer"* (Colossians 4:2).

But what does "pray without ceasing" actually mean? Constantly mumbling prayers to God from the moment you wake up till your head hits the pillow? That's hardly practical or attainable, especially when you are running around all day interacting with other people, taking care of your family, or buried in work. The practice of non-stop audible praying does exist, but only in some monastic orders. For instance, Russian and Eastern Orthodox monks softly recite prayers all day long while performing their daily duties, whether it is milking cows or cooking meals, or painting religious icons. But we are not monks, and we don't live in a monastic bubble separate from the world. We live in a fast-paced, real world with lots of distractions.

What, then, does "pray without ceasing" look like in the hubbub of everyday life? And why is it important?

Branches on a New Vine

To help us understand both the delight and duty of unceasing prayer, we need to take a closer look at what Jesus taught about what a relationship with Him as our Lord is supposed to look like:

"I am the true vine, and my Father is the vinedresser. Every branch in me that does not bear fruit he takes away, and every branch that does bear fruit he prunes, that it may bear more fruit. Already you are clean because of the word that I have spoken to you. Abide in me, and I in you. As the branch cannot bear fruit by itself, unless it abides in the vine, neither can you, unless you abide in me. I am the vine; you are the branches. Whoever abides in me and I in him, he it is that bears much fruit, for apart from me you can do nothing. If anyone does not abide in me he is thrown away like a branch and withers; and the branches are gathered, thrown into the fire, and burned. If you abide in me, and my words abide in you, ask whatever you wish, and it will be done for you. By this my Father is glorified, that you bear much fruit and so prove to be my disciples." (John 15:1-8)

As He often did, Jesus used an example from everyday first-century Jewish life, a vineyard. This example is about a branch that gets cut off from a weak vine and grafted into a healthy one. The vinedresser, or vintner, places the loose branch firmly against the new vine and binds it in place with strips of cloth that he then keeps wet for some time. Underneath the damp cloth, the branch begins to sprout tiny strands of fiber. Slowly they begin to latch on to the vine so that the branch can soak up life-giving sap, which strengthens it, gives it leaves, and eventually bears fruit. Sometime later, the vinedresser takes off the cloth strips to see if the branch has done its job of latching on and becoming one with the vine. If it hasn't, it will look dry and brittle and will fall off. At that point, he can't do anything with it but toss it in the fire. If it latched on, it would look green and healthy, firmly attached to the vine. The vinedresser can see that it has potential. As long as it stays connected with the vine, the branch will become enmeshed and bear lush, good fruit that will make the vintner proud.

Jesus' message is clear: attach yourself to me (abide in me) like a branch grafted to a new vine. It will allow you to soak up the fullness of the new life I give you, and you will bear much fruit for the Father's glory. *"Apart from Me, you can do nothing,"* He stresses. Not only that, but when you abide in Me, you may rest assured in the promise that the Father will answer your every prayer.

The implied warning is sobering: If you don't grab on to me, you will dry up spiritually, be fruitless, and be thrown away. Jesus implies that anyone who does not eventually show any sign of attaching firmly to Christ or even wanting to, and bearing visible fruit as evidence of a saved, changed life, most likely was not saved in the first place.

Unceasing prayer is key to latching on to the vine like a branch that is thirsty for life-giving sap. Constant communion with the Lord attaches us to Him and opens the way for Him to be involved in every aspect of our lives. Through our continuous abiding, He empowers us, enlightens us, guides us, directs us, corrects us, comforts us, emboldens us, and changes us. The attachment itself may not be outwardly visible to people. However, in the form of an increasingly Christlike character, the fruit it bears most definitely is. No one goes into a vineyard to admire the way a branch is attached to a vine. We just see the grapes and praise the vintner for his work. What remains hidden is that the secret to the quality of the grapes is the branch's attachment to the vine. That is precisely the way God wants it to be with us. Our attachment to the True Vine is closet stuff – away from the public eye. But the fruit our lives bear as a result of that attachment should be clearly visible to all – not to our glory, but God's.

Drudgery or Delight?

If I looked you in the eye and said, *"Friend, here is your most important assignment: Pray without ceasing,"* what would your reaction be? You might jump for joy at the delight of unbroken communion with God. Or you might think of it as drudgery – another thing to add to your already overflowing to-do list.

It would be drudgery if unceasing prayer were merely an obligation we had to fulfill to stay in good standing with God whether we feel like it or not. But that is never God's intention with any of the spiritual disciplines that help maintain a strong relationship with Him. Like any relationship, it should be driven by delight. That is part of loving someone. You want to be in their presence as much as you can, and you miss them when you can't.

The context of the command to pray without ceasing in 1 Thessalonians 5:17 helps us understand why it is intended as a delight rather than drudgery:

"Rejoice always, pray without ceasing, give thanks in all circumstances; for this is the will of God in Christ Jesus for you." (1 Thessalonians 5:16-18)

Being sandwiched between rejoicing and giving thanks paints a different picture of prayer without ceasing. That makes Paul's exhortation consistent with the blueprint Jesus gave us for prayer, in which supplication is mixed in with worship, adoration, and affirmation of God's glory.

Does this mean we have to be happy all the time and be thankful for everything, good and bad, or God won't be pleased with us? No, not quite. "Rejoice always" means to choose joy, even when sadness fills your heart. It says with the Psalmist:

"Why are you cast down, o my soul, and why are you in turmoil within me? Hope in God; for I shall again praise Him, my salvation and my God" (Psalm 42:5).

By choosing joy, we remind ourselves whenever we pray that God is in control, that He cares for us, that He loves us, that He has saved us, redeemed us, forgiven us, and destined us for heaven; That His presence is always near, and His peace and comfort always available. Your circumstances may suck, but God is always there to see you through. Think of it as the joy of Habakkuk:

"Though the fig tree should not blossom,
nor fruit be on the vines,
the produce of the olive fail
and the fields yield no food,
the flock be cut off from the fold
and there be no herd in the stalls,
yet I will rejoice in the LORD;
I will take joy in the God of my salvation."
(Habakkuk 3:17-18)

Like the sons of Korah who wrote Psalm 42 and the prophet Habakkuk, we choose joy in the presence of the Lord in the ups and downs of our lives and in His life flowing through us as we hold on to Him. We express that joy in unceasing communion with God.

To top it off, we give thanks in all circumstances for much the same reason. Instead of complaining to God when life gets tough, we give thanks because we know that in His hand, not a single difficulty or sorrow is wasted, and he is at work in all of them for our good (cf. Romans 8:29).

Perhaps now prayer without ceasing makes more sense. Through our joy of being in God's presence at all times, we draw Him into every aspect of our lives. That, in turn, overflows into being thankful in every circumstance. Sometimes the joy and gratitude may well up spontaneously. At other times it seems like a struggle, and we have to employ the kind of self-talk we saw in Psalm 42 in order to choose joy. But when we do, that joy and the desire to pray return. Our emotions follow our will, not the other way round.

I know that struggle all too well, even after I realized from my conversation with Dr. Sanders that our communion with God should be driven primarily by a desire for His presence rather than obligation or self-discipline. My personality has a negative side, which means I tend to see the manure in the barn before I see a pony. Sometimes all I see is manure! That, in turn, causes a tendency to complain rather than rejoice and give thanks in all circumstances. My freedom came from realizing that I can *choose* joy and gratitude rather than wait for my mood to get me there. Fortunately, God, in His endless patience, lets us pour out our hearts to Him in complaint. We can see that clearly in the Psalms and in Lamentations. However, He always wants us to return to joy and gratitude as our prayers' main flavoring. And He helps us when we struggle with that. In our darkest moments, He often sends us a tangible reminder that He is near, that He has heard our cry, and that salvation from our troubles is near. Such was the case with Victor Frankl, a former prisoner in a Nazi concentration camp during World War II. Almost his entire family perished in the gas chambers, and he lived in daily fear he might be next. He writes:

"In a last violent protest against the hopelessness of imminent death, I sensed my spirit piercing through the enveloping gloom. I felt it transcend that hopeless, meaningless world, and from somewhere I heard a victorious 'Yes' in answer to my question of the existence of an ultimate purpose. At that moment a light was lit in a distant farmhouse, which stood on the horizon as if painted there, in the midst of the miserable grey of a dawning morning in Bavaria. 'Et lux in tenebris lucent'--and the light shineth in the darkness." [1]

If you find yourself amid feelings of drudgery and depression instead of delight, and it seems impossible to rejoice, reading the Psalms or biographies of those who learned from their struggles may help. So does being honest with yourself before God. Don't ignore or suppress your battle. God already knows what is in your heart, so express it instead. When you do, He comes to your aid. Like He did with Viktor Frankl amid his unimaginable suffering. As He did with David in the caves and Elijah in the desert, God will send you a reminder to lift your spirits and restore you to a place of always rejoicing and giving thanks in all circumstances. And that puts you right back at the center of His will.

Habit or Relationship?

Prayer without ceasing is a command that can lead you down the wrong path when taken out of context. Believe it or not, it is possible to establish daily prayer habits and completely lose sight of the relationship with Christ. What is the difference, you might ask? A habit serves *you*, whereas a relationship serves *Christ*. Let me explain.

Many of the world's major religions emphasize rigorous routines of spiritual exercises. I remember going into Buddhist temples in Singapore for a school project and interviewing Buddhist monks about their lives. I asked about why they spent so much time in silent meditation and mindlessly reciting prayers. Their answers unequivocally stated that those disciplines were essential for their well-being. They had no personal relationship with Buddha. I have heard the same from Muslims and even Jews. Their five-times-a-day prayers- prescribed, recited, and unspontaneous- are an attempt at following rules and, at best, trying to please the godhead they are praying to. Again, no relationship. No direct sense of connection or intimacy with God.

Similarly, it is possible for us to attach more importance to following a daily habit than having a relationship with God. I have caught myself doing that many times because I tend to be a creature of habit. I love routines. I like habits. But after a while, I began to notice that I had more of a desire to get my devotional ritual out of the way first so I could get on with other things. I wasn't really looking forward to meeting with God. I would rush through the familiar elements of what I considered a quiet time alone with God, skim through a devotional book or a few Bible verses, say a hasty prayer to commit my day to the Lord, and ask Him to help me through it. Then I would jump up, happy to be done. Looking at that from God's perspective, it must have felt like the spiritual version of trying to spend time with someone who is constantly checking their smartphone while you're trying to have a conversation. That person may leave your get-together with the satisfaction of having fulfilled their promise to meet, but it leaves you empty, unvalued, and dissatisfied.

Prayer habits are good in as far as they are the expression of a heart that loves God and a mind set on the things of His Kingdom. But He is not looking for us to merely have prayer habits and be good at them. He wants a *relationship* with us. Prayer without ceasing is useless if it is not a framework for a two-way communion with God in which we speak and listen with a grateful heart that rejoices in His presence. We have to pay attention that we don't love our spiritual habits more than we love God. Believe it or not, our prayer life can become an idol in itself and stand in the way of a relationship with our heavenly Father. We can either become proud of our habit, which isn't good since God opposes the proud (James 4:6), or walk around with "evangeliguilt" – a sense of self-condemnation over not being consistent with our daily routine.

An Attitude of Prayer

Prayer without ceasing, while rejoicing in God and giving thanks in all circumstances, amounts to having an *attitude of prayer*. Nineteenth-century pastor and author E.M. Bounds, known for his books on prayer, describes an attitude of prayer like this:

"There are, and ought to be, set seasons if communion with God, when everything else is shut out and we come into His presence to talk to Him and let Him speak to us. And out of such seasons will spring that beautiful habit of prayer that weaves a

golden bond between earth and heaven. Without these seasons of prayer, set as a pattern for our lives, the habit of prayer can never be formed; without them, there is no nourishment of the spiritual life." [2]

A life-long pattern of regular prayer times - motivated by a desire to be in God's presence during which we talk and listen to God as He nourishes us - produces in us an attitude of prayer we carry with us throughout the day. They go together like a horse and carriage.

J. Oswald Sanders, the same who opened my eyes to the importance of needing to have a desire to meet with God, spoke at a missionary prayer group my wife and I were privileged to host many years later. He said that the secret to an attitude of prayer lies in how we use our discretionary time. It turns out we spend quite a bit of time in idle mode throughout our day, probably more than we realize.

Some research backs him up. According to a Timex survey of how much people in the US spend waiting, people wait on average 20 minutes a day for the bus or train, 32 minutes whenever they visit a doctor, and 28 minutes standing in security lines when they travel. Those of us lucky enough to be in a love relationship wait 21 minutes for a significant other to get ready to go out. Additionally, we spend some 13 hours a year remaining on hold for customer service, reports Timex. According to the Atlantic Newspaper, the average commuter spends 38 hours a year waiting in traffic. Big city commuters average more than 50 hours waiting in traffic annually. [3]. That does not include time spent driving back and forth to work, standing in lines in banks and stores, walking from one place to another, or lunch and coffee breaks. All in all, we spend on average about 3 hours a day in idle mode, which is what Mr. Sanders called "discretionary time."

If you're a fidget like me, you'll fill that time up with all sorts of things. Mostly entertainment. We crank up the radio while driving or waiting in traffic, we let our minds wander, or we people-watch while we stand in line or walk from one place to another, and most of us engage in a love affair with that dopamine dispenser we call a smartphone every opportunity we get. There go our break times. To underscore the latter, surveys conducted in 2020 by tech websites concluded that the average smartphone user (which is 272.6 million in the US alone) interacts with his or her phone 64-86 times daily for an average screen time of 5.4 hours. Agreed, some of that is useful. But let's be honest, a lot of it is not.

Those discretionary moments in our day provide an excellent opportunity to stay connected with God and foster the attitude of constant prayer He desires for us. God, after all, is omnipresent. He is with you in the car, at work, in the grocery store, while you are waiting or taking breaks. And He is accessible 24/7. His throne is open for business 365 days out of the year—three sixty-six in leap years.

While your extended time in the prayer closet allows Him to truly minister to your soul, your frequent checking in with Him throughout the day fosters an unbroken awareness of His presence that makes it easy to pause and pray at any given moment. It doesn't have to be deep or elaborate. It doesn't require you to sit somewhere quiet where you can close your eyes, drop to your knees, and pour your heart out. It can be just a simple prayer of praise and thanksgiving as you see the beauty of the sky or sense the warmth of His presence while you drive or walk. It can be a quick request for help as you encounter an issue or see someone in need. For instance, I have heard of several people who have gotten in the habit of pausing for a quick prayer every time they see or hear an emergency vehicle. Others respond to news alerts of emergencies, disasters, or tragedies with prayer.

I speak from personal experience when I say that using those discretionary moments for prayer is worth gold. There have been days when I left God behind in the prayer closet, closed the door on my way to work, and barely thought of Him throughout my day. Those days didn't turn out so well. And regaining a sense of His presence the next day was much more challenging as He seemed a million miles away.

But just as I like to think of my wife during idle moments in my day and text her when I can, I have learned to check in with God the same way – minus the texting. I drive a lot for my day job, and for me driving means praying. I turn the radio off or play soft instrumental music and talk out loud to God. I used to be self-conscious about this, but nowadays, you see many drivers talk aloud in their cars while using their hands-free phones, so it doesn't look weird anymore. And even if it did, I wouldn't care. I am on the phone with God!

James 4:8 tells us to *"draw near to God, and he will draw near to you."* Using those discretionary times to draw near to God, however briefly, results in God drawing near to us and making His presence known. It keeps the channels open for Him to give us promptings, wisdom, insights, and encouragements.

During the years I served as a jail chaplain, the command staff told me to develop a "radio ear." All staff members not seated at a desk were connected to a command center via portable radios. While going about my duties, whether it was one-on-one counseling with inmates, distributing Bibles, or reorganizing our library, I always had to keep one ear tuned to the radio in case they needed me. Drawing near to God kind of works that way, too. As we go about our day, we stay tuned in to the presence of God, whatever we're doing. More concentrated times of focus during our idle moments help strengthen that awareness. We develop as it were a spiritual "radio ear" – a constant, almost subconscious, receptivity to the presence and voice of God. And as we listen and receive what He gives us throughout the day, His impartation and the sheer awareness of His closeness deepen our joy and strengthen our peace no matter what the day brings. Doing this also keeps our appetite for the things of God alive. When we nibble at the table of the world all day long through our interaction with it and neglect eating from God's table, we eventually lose our appetite for His presence and the spiritual truths of His kingdom. Then the relationship fades, and it takes a lot of effort, repentance, and re-learning the things of the Spirit to get it back to where it was.

Devoted to Prayer

Like consistent communication and togetherness in any love relationship, prayer without ceasing does take work. That is where delight and duty go hand in hand. The delight part keeps your heart focused on what you want, namely fellowship with the God you love and Who is everything to you. The duty part helps you do the work necessary to pursue what you want, namely, remove the distractions we discussed, make time, free up your mind to focus on God, and intentionally use your discretionary time to stay connected to Him.

This "duty" is what the Bible calls devotion. In Acts 2:42, we read, *"and they devoted themselves to the apostles' teaching and the fellowship, to the breaking of bread and the prayers."*

But what exactly is devotion? *The Merriam-Webster Dictionary* defines it as "the fact or state of being ardently dedicated and loyal." [4] *The American Heritage Dictionary of the English Language* calls it "ardent, often selfless affection and dedication, as to a person or principle." [5] *Strong's Exhaustive Concordance* defines devotion directly from the Greek word proskartereó. Literally, that means "strong toward". Figuratively, it means "to attend assiduously" or "to be constantly diligent" [6]. Jesus described devotion to the Kingdom of God with a word picture:

"The kingdom of heaven is like treasure hidden in a field, which a man found and covered up. Then in his joy he goes and

sells all that he has and buys that field" (Matthew 13:44).

Ardent. Selfless. Dedication. Sacrificing all that one has. That is true devotion to something we consider priceless to have. And there is nothing more priceless than God. He created us, went to the cross for us, rescued us, forgave us, redeemed us, filled, sealed, and gifted us with His Spirit, teaches us, provides for us, protects us, guides us, comforts us, strengthens us, changes us, and keeps us on a heavenward course. Nothing says *"I love you, Lord"* louder than ardent devotion to unceasing prayer. Nothing screams *"I don't care"* louder than neglecting it. The saying goes that actions speak louder than words. A profession of love for God means nothing if we don't show it by consistent efforts to sweep our distractions aside and make our daily walk with Him our top priority in the way we live.

We encounter that in our human relationships as well. It is one thing to tell your wife that you love her. It is another thing to demonstrate that love by listening, caring, sacrificing your interests (like watching sports or going fishing with the guys), and helping her when she is tired. Or by spending money to buy her flowers just to say that she means the world to you. Which of the two speaks louder in your marriage: your profession of love or your demonstration of love?

Many marriages die from neglect more than conflict. The same goes for the greatest and deepest love relationship a human can have – fellowship with God. The difference between occasional communication and constant connection reminds me of the difference between an electrical appliance and a wind-up toy. When you plug, say, a toaster into an outlet and keep it plugged in, you have constant power flowing to it. All you have to do is pop in a piece of bread and depress the lever, and voila, it heats up and toasts the bread without you even having to think about it. You just assume it works because it is plugged in.

A wind-up toy, on the other hand, will require considerable

79

effort to get to full tension. Once you put it on the ground to enjoy what it does, it will go full tilt for a few moments, then quickly peter out until you wind it up again.

As easily distracted Christians, a lot of us are winder-uppers. We go to a service or small group, some conference or meeting, and we get fired up about our relationship with the Lord. Then we get back home to the distractions, the to-dos, and demands that are always there, and our excitement about the Lord, prayer, Bible reading, and ministry quickly dissipates - unless we have learned the secret of staying plugged into our heavenly Power Source.

Duty and devotion to staying connected to the Vine are our sole responsibility as Christians. He does everything else in us and for us. In God's eyes, our unceasing prayer is most valuable if it comes from a desire for Him and delight in His Presence, rather than a sense of indebtedness or obligation.

Prayer without ceasing is essential to letting the fullness of His life fully develop in us. It is the golden thread between heaven and earth that E.M. Bounds wrote about - the thread that weaves our spiritual life with our earthly life. It is worth every effort of our will, any sacrifice, any battle against distractions from within and without. It is key to our spiritual growth and His pleasure in us. It is vital to the success of any ministry He engages us in, and it is the only way to bear fruit for His glory.

Neglecting the delight and duty of unceasing prayer grieves God. It stagnates our spiritual growth. It causes us to feel far away from God and fruitless in ministry. It opens the door for Satan to keep his dominion over us and beset us with depression, anxiety, inner turmoil, and unnecessary toil.

The commands to be devoted to prayer, constant in prayer, persist in prayer, and to pray without ceasing are ultimately for our good. Nothing pleases God more than to see His children express their love for Him in word and deed. And there we find that the things which please God the most benefit us the most in return.

Prayer Practice

We talked about idle moments throughout your day. We saw how important they are to maintaining an attitude of prayer, assuming you have already created a pattern of regular extended quiet times in your personal prayer space. With that in mind, this chapter's Prayer Practice has two parts to it.

1. Keep a journal of your daily discretionary time for five days. In whichever way you find it easiest, record when you had idle moments and how long those moments lasted. They could be time spent driving, waiting in line, sitting in traffic, walking between places, or taking breaks. Add up how many minutes, or hours, a day you spent in idle mode. An optional addition would be to record what you did during those idle moments.

2. Begin using as many of those idle times for prayer. Turn off the car radio, keep your phone in your pocket, and direct your mind to God. Just talk to Him in silent prayer. Begin small – tell Him you love Him, tell Him thanks for your blessings. Then add specifics. Ask Him to put things on your heart to pray for during those idle times.

   - Perhaps a colleague or a friend.
   - Perhaps for an emergency as you hear an ambulance.
   - Pray for a church as you drive by.
   - Ask His help for a problem you face at work.

3. The possibilities are endless. And when distractions get the better of you, ask God to help you focus on Him. He always does because He wants you to.

Soon you will find that God does not seem far away at all, and it is easy to sense His presence wherever you are. And the more you feel His presence, the easier it becomes to pray without ceasing.

Questions For Reflection And Discussion

1. When you hear the command "pray without ceasing," does that make you think of delight or drudgery? Why?

2. What is the relationship between duty, delight, and devotion?

3. What are some of the key ingredients of an unbroken relationship with God?

Chapter 6
Praying To Please God

We have learned quite a bit about powerful and effective prayer so far. Now we come to our next step: learning to pray in a way that pleases God.

Two prayer dynamics matter a great deal to Him: praying with *faith* and praying with the *right motive*. Neither one is as complicated or scary as they sound. They are not unfamiliar to us since they are critical to any human relationship as well. We know them perhaps better as *trust* and *sincerity*. To foster a strong relationship, whether it is a marriage, a close friendship, or a tight-knit work relationship, we have to have mutual trust, and we have to be sincere and honest. The quickest way to ruin a relationship is to betray another's trust or to be insincere in what we say or do. As soon as that gets found out, the person at the short end of the stick feels betrayed or used and will most likely be unable to trust you again unless you have corrected yourself and repaired the damage. As the relationship grows, you get to know each other so well that it becomes almost impossible to get away with anything insincere or dishonest that you know will violate your bond and hurt the other person.

Not that we could ever know the depths of God. Only the Holy Spirit can (1 Corinthians 2:10-12). But He does know our depths. In fact, He knows them better than we do:

"O LORD, you have searched me and known me! You know when I sit down and when I rise up; you discern my thoughts from afar. You search out my path and my lying down and are acquainted with all my ways. Even before a word is on my tongue, behold, O LORD, you know it altogether." (Psalm 139:1-4).

When we approach God in prayer, we have to be aware that

He knows our every thought, every fear, every doubt, every hope, every dream, every desire before we ever express it in prayer. He knows full well whether or not we are praying with faith or out of unbelief and if we pray with the right motive.

That is both scary and liberating. It is scary in the sense that we can't get away with anything. It is liberating in the sense that out of God's omniscience, He lovingly and graciously helps us overcome the sinful nature that undermines our faith and corrupts our motive.

Faith Pleases God

The Bible is very clear about how important our faith is to God. Hebrews 11 – a chapter dedicated entirely to the subject of faith – says in vs. 6: *"And without faith it is impossible to please Him (God), for whoever would draw near to God must believe that He exists and that He rewards those who seek Him."*

Without faith it is *impossible* to please God. Whoever draws near (prays) *must* believe. At the bare minimum, that He exists. At the very least, that He rewards you for seeking Him. There is something worth knowing about the words "seek" and "reward." The Greek word for "seek" (ekzētousin) means "to search for" or "to crave." The term "rewards" (misthapodotēs – literally: become a rewarder) means "renumerates." That is significant because it essentially means that God rewards our craving for Him with an equivalent level of attention to our requests.

There is a direct relationship between faith and craving. We crave what we trust will meet our needs. When we are thirsty, we crave water because we have faith that it will alleviate that thirst. We have experienced it before, and that experience has made our faith that water will quench our thirst stronger. Moreover, we have discovered that water tastes good, making our craving even more potent.

In the same way, we believe that God is our Creator, Savior,

Redeemer, Provider, Protector, Father, among many other things, and that He is more than able to meet our needs. That trust makes us hungry for Him and His help. Then as we taste His presence and experience His answers to our prayers, that taste of His goodness makes us want Him and trust Him even more. That combination of desire and faith pleases Him greatly.

The absence of faith not only displeases God, but it is also a surefire way to see your prayers go unanswered. James elaborates on that:

"If any of you lacks wisdom, let him ask God, who gives generously to all without reproach, and it will be given him. But let him ask in faith, with no doubting, for the one who doubts is like a wave of the sea that is driven and tossed by the wind. For that person must not suppose that he will receive anything from the Lord; he is a double-minded man, unstable in all his ways." (James 1:5-8)

In other words: if you don't ask in faith, don't expect to receive anything from the Lord because doubt suggests doublemindedness, and that does not please God. More about that later.

What is Faith?

Faith is confusing for many. It seems abstract, difficult to understand, and challenging to gain or increase. It is not uncommon for someone to despair over not receiving an answer to prayer and get counsel from well-meaning brothers and sisters to "have more faith." I have been at the receiving end of that and tried to conjure up more of that thing called faith without result, so I know what that feels like. Others may have heard people who testified that God rewarded their faith for tangible things like miracles of healing, provision of large amounts of money, or a job change. They feel inadequate because God did not seem to do the same things for them. It raises questions like: Is my faith lacking? Am I really saved and have an "in" with God? Did I sin in some way that God didn't give me the desires of my heart? Does He love me less than the person who seems to get all his prayers answered? Hardly the stuff you can build trust in God on.

So, what exactly is faith? The Bible has a precise definition: *"Faith now is the assurance of things hoped for, the conviction of things not seen."* (Hebrews 11:1)

Another way of putting it is that you are confident that what you hope for will come to pass and you are convinced that the things you can't see are real.

It is important to understand that there is a difference between natural faith and spiritual faith. Every human being has the innate capacity to have faith, but it is limited chiefly to trusting material things – things we can see, hear, smell, or touch. When you mail a letter, you do so in faith that the postal service will get it to its correct destination. When you get in a car, you believe that it will get you from a to b without breaking down. When you board an airplane, you entrust your life to pilots in faith that they are skilled to get you there safely and that the plane has been sufficiently serviced to ensure it won't crash. Much of our everyday life is built around faith in systems, gizmos, gadgets, transportation modes, goods, and services.

The kind of faith the Bible talks about – the assurance of things hoped for and the conviction of things not seen – is spiritual faith. It goes beyond trust in what we can observe with our senses. It is a trust, a conviction, in what – or rather Who – we cannot see. It is a way of seeing the unseen and the Unseen One.

Spiritual faith has an entry point, a root, an object, and a growth trajectory.

The *entry point* is hearing and not just hearing anything. Hearing the Word of God, which we know to be living and active. Romans 10:17 says: *"So faith comes from hearing, and hearing through the word of Christ."* That goes for our initial faith that the gospel of Jesus was true when we heard it and for every subsequent hearing of God's Word. Our initial response to the hearing of God's Word was a sense of conviction that we needed to be reconciled to God through Jesus Christ. We came to Him in repentance and surrender. We received forgiveness of sins, redemption, adoption into God's household. The Holy Spirit to indwell us, faith in the reality of God's existence, of our salvation and newfound righteousness through the atonement of Christ, of His love for us and His engagement with our daily lives, came to us as a gift. Our human nature cannot conjure up that kind of faith. It is awakened in our spiritual nature by the Holy Spirit for the specific purpose of perceiving and understanding spiritual truths (see 1 Corinthians 2:14-16).

Once faith is planted in us by the Holy Spirit as God's gift, it needs to get *rooted* in devotion to the truth, authority, and infallibility of the Word of God. That happens when we hear (which includes reading), study, believe, and apply it. The text in Romans 10:17 implies this. Embrace the Word of Christ, and your spirit is infused with faith. Neglect the Word, and your faith will grow dim. The Word reveals the unseen God to us – His attributes, His thoughts, His plans, His ways, His design for our lives. The more we see of Him, the stronger our faith in Him grows.

Perhaps most importantly, our faith has an *object*. Or rather, an Object, with a capital O. I am sure you've heard it said: *"My faith is not big, but I have faith in a big God."* That may sound like a platitude, but it harbors a vital truth. The greatness of the Person you have faith in is more important than the size of your faith.

But didn't Jesus get frustrated repeatedly with His disciples' lack of faith? (Matthew 17:20, Mark 4:40, Mark 6:6, Luke 8:25) And didn't he tell them that *"if you had faith like a grain of mustard seed, you could say to this mulberry tree 'Be uprooted and planted in the sea,' and it would obey you?"* (Luke 17:6). Didn't Jesus say that the size of a person's faith does matter? He did, but not as if faith is a thing that grows by itself. The lack of faith of the disciples betrayed too dim of a view of God and His power. Hence the almost sarcastic 'if you had faith the size of a mustard seed.' Because faith is our way to see God, it focuses our heart on His greatness and His grace toward us who seek Him.

As a result, our faith does have a *growth trajectory*. The more we get to know God, the more our faith in Him grows. That happens in two ways: first, we get to know God through His Word. As we study it and meditate on it, the Holy Spirit helps us see His glory and not just a bunch of information (Psalm 119:18). Then, as we seek Him and see Him answer our prayers, the experience of His engagement with us helps grow our faith in Him. The more we learn about Him, the clearer and greater He becomes to us, and the easier it is to have faith in Him.

I have watched a couple of seasons of a TV program that features helicopter rescues by the United States Coast Guard of boaters in distress from their sinking vessels in rough waters. It is spectacular to watch. They hover over or near a ship in distress in response to a mayday call, cool as cucumbers. A rescue swimmer is lowered down on a cable. He attaches the survivors to that cable or puts them in a basket, after which they are hoisted up to the safety of the helicopter. After the rescue, the TV crew interviews the survivors. You will hear them say: *"I thought we were goners, but when we heard the buzz of a helicopter, we knew that help was coming. Once we saw a familiar orange shape overhead and a rescue swimmer coming down to get us, we knew we were safe."*

The sound and sight of the approaching helicopter birthed hope and seeing the rescuer being lowered down caused their hope to grow into the assurance that they would make it. So much so that they would gladly follow any direction from the rescuers. Jump off the ship in our survival suits? Sure! Swim in 30-foot swells towards the basket? Sure! Letting you guys hoist me up 80 feet while swinging wildly in mid-air? Sure! Because we know you do this all the time. We know you are professionals. We know that the big helicopter will hold steady in the howling wind. We know that we will be safe.

That is perhaps a good illustration of how our faith grows. We hear it. We realize God's Word is true as the Holy Spirit whispers to our soul. We embrace it. Then we root ourselves in it. We make our mayday calls for help based on what we have learned about Him. We watch Him come to our aid and work in our lives. And the more we know about Him and experience Him, the more our faith in Him grows until our confidence in the Unseen becomes unshakeable, and the substance of our hope becomes concrete.

An important aspect of the way our faith grows is testing. James talks about that.

"Count it all joy, my brothers, when you meet trials of various kinds, for you know that the testing of your faith produces steadfastness" (James 1:2,3).

Trials of various kinds – hassle, problems, setbacks, disasters, great and small, taunt us to believe that God can solve them or bring good out of them. But the more we bring Him into those trials and see what He does with them, the stronger our faith in Him becomes. It is not unlike going to the gym. The more you push yourself and test your muscles against the resistance of weights or cardio machines, the stronger your body becomes.

Faith is not an abstract force that comes and goes or that you can conjure up to do heroic things. Faith is a gift from God to us. It is a Holy Spirit-enabled way of correctly seeing spiritual truths, and especially the One Who is the Truth. That is why it pleases Him.

I Believe, Help Me In My Unbelief!

If faith is a gift from God to help you see Him with spiritual eyes, what then is the opposite of faith? Is it unbelief? Or doubt? Or both?

Perhaps what you have read so far is making you take stock of your faith, and you find yourself echoing the father of a demon-possessed boy after he watched Jesus set him free: *"I believe! Help me in my unbelief!"* (Mark 9:24). He said that after Jesus challenged his initial skepticism and told him that all things are possible for one who believes. It was a cry of repentance since he realized that he had come to Jesus with his request after he had tried it out on the disciples first, who couldn't help him. The words *"if you can do anything, have compassion and help us"* (Mark 9:22) bespeak kind of a last-hope desperation move.

This father's mindset was initially one of distrust, which is what the word unbelief in the Greek (apistia) means. He had perhaps not yet known enough about Jesus to realize His authority. Or maybe he had become cynical after his followers couldn't drive out the demon. The good news is that Jesus worked despite the father's unbelief and not only healed his child but helped him realize that he needed Jesus to help him have faith.

God is compassionate and patient with us. He already knows when we have trouble believing Him for an answer to our prayers. We might as well fess up then and ask God to help us move from unbelief to belief. In response to our confession, God will come to our aid. Sometimes by answering our prayer, as Jesus did with the father, to prove that our unbelief was unfounded so that we might learn from it. Often, He helps us see things differently. What looked hopeless at first now looks like an opportunity for God to show His grace and His power.

There is another opposite of faith – one that presents a different problem with another solution. Again, we turn to James:

"But let him ask in faith, with no doubting, for the one who doubts is like a wave of the sea that is driven and tossed by the wind. For that person must not suppose that he will receive anything from the Lord; he is a double-minded man, unstable in all his ways." (James 1:6-8).

You can argue that doubt is a form of unbelief, but there is more to it than that. While the Greek word for unbelief (apistia) denotes distrust, the term used for doubt in James 1:6 comes from the root diakrino, which means "to judge,' "to oppose," or "to discriminate." He goes on to say that such a person is double-minded and unstable. It is one thing to have trouble believing that God will answer a specific prayer, especially perhaps for something big. It is another to be double-minded and unstable, because now you are talking about something deeper: a person's outlook on life. If doubting comes from double-mindedness and instability, it means that a doubter still has a perspective that is in part unspiritual and worldly. And the Bible is clear that worldliness and faith in God are at odds with each other. James, again:

"You adulterous people! Do you not know that friendship with the world is enmity with God? Therefore whoever wishes to be a friend of the world makes himself an enemy of God." (James 4:4).

That is a whole different problem. Now we have someone who doesn't have trouble believing God for a significant issue but who has a mindset that is trying to stay friends with the world and with God at the same time. He has one leg in the world and the other in the kingdom of God and can't bring himself to move the one leg over. James calls that adultery. Ouch! Keeping at least in part a worldly outlook, which is all about personal prestige and gain, clouds his view of God. It also hampers his faith in God. Perhaps it makes him want God to answer prayer his way instead of God's way. A prayer cried out in unbelief is heard because the pray-er's heart is right. A prayer prayed in double-mindedness is not heard because his heart isn't right.

Such was the case in a parable Jesus told His disciples about a tax collector and a Pharisee. They both went up to the temple to pray. The Pharisee thanked God that he wasn't like the unjust, extortioners, adulterers, or even like this tax collector he was standing next to. Then he reminded God that he fasted twice a week and gave tithes of all his income. Talk about personal prestige and gain and a clouded view of God! The tax collector, on the other hand, wouldn't even lift his eyes to heaven but beat his chest and cried out for God to be merciful to him, a sinner. You can read the whole story in Luke 18:9-14. The lesson? Both men prayed, but only the prayer of one was answered. You can guess which one.

Unbelief can stand in the way of God answering a prayer. Doubt, as a symptom of double-mindedness, stands in the way of receiving anything from God at all. That is far more serious.

Moving from unbelief to faith requires an honest cry for help. Moving from doubt and double-mindedness to faith requires humble soul searching and repentance – a drastic change of heart away from worldliness and toward godliness; surrender to God's will in the answers to one's prayer instead of trying to exert one's own will. Or as James puts it:

"Submit yourselves therefore to God. Resist the devil, and he will flee from you. Draw near to God, and he will draw near to you. Cleanse your hands, you sinners, and purify your hearts, you double-minded. Be wretched and mourn and weep. Let your laughter be turned to mourning and your joy to gloom. Humble yourselves before the Lord, and he will exalt you." (James 5:7-9).

Motive Matters

To please God, we have to pray with faith, but we also have to pray with the right motive. James has a few choice words about that as well: *"You do not have, because you do not ask. You ask and do not receive, because you ask wrongly, to spend it on your passions"* (James 4:2b,3).

The verses that follow place that statement in the context of a worldly mindset. Look at it as a cause-and-effect chain reaction: A Christian's friendship with the world causes him to pray with a selfish motive, which in turn causes him not to receive an answer.

The reason he gives is that friendship with the world is enmity with God. Apparently, it is possible to be a Christian and still live, at least in part, as an enemy with God. And God is not satisfied until we are sanctified through and through (1 Thessalonians 5:23) until all areas of aversion to Him are driven out of the deepest recesses of our being, and we are single-mindedly devoted to Him.

Praying with the right motive is important because it relates to the divine design that Jesus gave us, namely that we align ourselves with His will. That is what "your kingdom come, your will be done" means. It is also the caveat to the promise of answered prayer.

In 1 John 5:14, 15, we see, *"And this is the confidence we have toward Him, that if we ask anything according to His will He hears us. And if we know that He hears us in whatever we ask, we know that we have the requests we ask of Him."*

So, the 'whatever we ask of Him' has to be qualified requests –according to His will and for our personal gratification.

I've heard prosperity preachers talk about James 4 and use the phrase *"you do not have because you do not ask"* as a blank check to ask anything you want from God. Especially health, wealth, and personal success. That sounds so appealing, especially if you are poor or struggling in some way. Why wouldn't a God who loves me want me to be wealthy? Well...because love of material wealth is friendship with the world, and therefore enmity with God. The riches He wants us to pray for is spiritual riches. And the motive for our prayers that please Him is that we seek His glory and not ours.

The difference between seeking the will and the glory of God and wanting something for our own gratification can be very subtle. I have found myself praying that God would increase the number of monthly donors to our ministry and then got frustrated that the number went down instead of up. As I set about trying to discover the reason why my prayer, which seemed perfectly legit, wasn't answered, the Holy Spirit shone His light of conviction into my heart where I stumbled across the desire to have financial security out of a fear of lack. I realized that God wanted me to trust Him completely, as I claimed I did, for month-by-month provision. It is easy to think that you do while you have a large reserve in the bank. It is another thing to say that you trust God while you're down to just a couple of dollars with bills due the next day. I realized that God's will for me was to grow my faith in Him. My will for me was to be financially secure.

I have learned over the years – slowly because I can be dense – that frustration with God over unanswered prayer often is an indicator of praying with the wrong motive. God's design for us is to pray in surrender to every aspect of His will. That includes the answer itself, when it comes, and the way that it comes. Sometimes the answer is no. At that point, we have to accept that Father knows best, and as a good father, He gives us what we need and not what we want. At times, an answer to prayer comes quickly, and at other times it takes much longer, even years. We have to trust that God, in His wisdom, chooses the ideal time for the perfect answer.

And then there is the problem of expectation. Whenever we present a request to God, we are tempted to imagine how He will answer. Perhaps you prayed about a financial need, and you began to expect that God would stir the hearts of certain people to help you. They did not; you got frustrated, only to discover that the answer suddenly appears from somewhere you least expected. You may have heard the made-up story of a man stuck on the roof of his house during a flood. With the water rapidly rising, he cries out to God to come and rescue him. A few minutes later, the fire department shows up and throws him a lifesaver. But he waves them off, saying: *"God will rescue me!"* Sometime later, a fisherman passes by his house in a boat. He sees the man and yells for him to hop in. Again, he waves him off. With the water still rising and almost to his feet, a Coast Guard helicopter (who else!) spots him and lowers a basket for him to get in and be lifted off. But he waves them off as well, yelling: *"God is going to rescue me!"* Eventually, though, the water engulfs his house, swallows him up, and he drowns. As he arrives in heaven, he comes face-to-face with the Lord. Indignantly, he asks: *"why did you not rescue me and let me die instead?"* The Lord replies: *"I did. I sent you a fire truck, a boat, and a helicopter, but you refused them all."*

The moral of this story is, we must not box God in by our expectations of when and how He will answer. Those expectations come all too often from the desire for instant gratification or to have some form of control. Both stem from our sinful nature that wants self-determination. In reality, they are subtle forms of worldly double-mindedness and out of sync with wholeheartedly saying, *"your will be done."*

Over time, we learn to recognize whether or not we are praying with the right motive. That is part of the value of what we learned in Chapter 3, that the Holy Spirit helps us in our weakness because we do not know what we ought to pray for. Learning to ask Him to help us pray ensures that we pray according to His will and with the right motive. When our motive isn't right, the Holy Spirit doesn't give us the words. Instead, He pricks us in our conscience that something is out of kilter. We discover what it is because He helps us see it, and we learn that it is impossible to have true faith in anything outside the scope of God's will. Once you see your mistake, you can correct yourself because God is pleased when you pray with the right motive - out of love for Him and not of the world, in surrender to His will, and desiring Him to be glorified in the answer.

Praying Like Elijah

One of the most encouraging passages in Scripture regarding praying with faith is in James 5:16b-18:

"The prayer of a righteous person has great power as it is working. Elijah was a man with a nature like ours, and he prayed fervently that it might not rain, and for three years and six months it did not rain on the earth. Then he prayed again, and heaven gave rain, and the earth bore its fruit."

Some translations say, *"The prayer of a righteous person is powerful and effective."* It will, for instance, rescue a sin-sick person from his bondage (vs. 14,15). James seems to imply that lack of faith was an issue for the recipients of his letter. He encourages them by saying that the prophet Elijah, who was with Jesus on the Mount of Transfiguration and will be one of God's witnesses in the End Times, was a human being just like us. So, he recounts the story of Elijah out of 1 King 18, where at God's command, he prayed for it to stop raining. After three and a half years of drought and famine, he prays for it to start raining again. There are a couple of details worth noting in that story.

First, Elijah prayed under definite instruction from God to pray a specific prayer. So he knew he prayed according to God's will. Secondly, when he prayed for it to start raining again, he had to persevere in that prayer because his servant, who he sent to look for an answer, kept coming back with negative reports. Seven times, as a matter of fact. Both times, God answered his prayers. Elijah's prayer is a model of praying with faith and praying with the right motive. And James says: you are just like him, so be encouraged!

Some might stumble over the word "righteous" as in *"the prayer of a righteous man is powerful and effective."* They think, "but I'm not righteous. At least not as righteous as Elijah. Wrong!

We are righteous in Christ. In response to our repentance and baptism, our sins have been forgiven, and we received the gift of righteousness (Romans 5:17). It was purchased for us by the blood of Jesus Christ on the cross. The righteousness God gave us is perfect and can't be tarnished by anything, as opposed to any sort of righteousness we try to achieve by ourselves. God will not hear our prayers based on whether we have behaved well, are basically good people, or are practically perfect in every way. He hears us because we are righteous *in Christ*. According to what we just read in the Bible, that makes our prayer both powerful and effective. As powerful and effective as Elijah's. Just. Wow!

So be encouraged. Praying to please God is easier than it sounds! He helps us grow our faith and confront any seeds of unbelief or doubt. And He helps us pray according to His will and for His glory. He delights in such prayers, and He wants them to be powerful and effective.

Prayer Practice

Ask the Lord for two things:

1. *To shine His light on any areas where you have had trouble believing that He will answer your prayers and show you why.* Write down your findings in your journal as a reminder for later, and confess them to Him. Then ask Him to help you overcome those areas of unbelief.

For example: For many years, I had trouble believing that God would answer prayers for personal needs like financial provision when we were short on money (which happens in ministry, believe it or not). I knew He was able to. I just had a hard time believing that He was willing to do that for me. When I asked Him to help me in my unbelief, I started to see that it had a root. I was basing my prayers on believing whether or not I was worthy of an answer and not on the finished work of Christ through which I had received the gift of righteousness and was worthy, entirely apart from my own doing. That freed me to believe, to ask, and to receive.

2. *To shine His light on your motive in praying for certain things.* Did you pray them out of a selfish desire rather than wanting God to get the glory? Did you try to exert your will on God because you struggle with giving up control instead of submitting to His plans and purposes? Write down your findings in your journal as well, and ask the Lord to make you sensitive to the Holy Spirit pricking your conscience to correct you.

Questions For Reflection And Discussion

1. Has someone ever told you to "have more faith" when you confided in them about prayers that went unanswered? How did that make you feel? What do you think is wrong, and what is right, about that statement?

2. Think back to any prayer request that God did not grant (bearing in mind that He always answers our prayers, but sometimes the answer is "no" or "not now.") Do you think it might have been due to the motive for your prayer, or another reason?

3. There is great freedom in understanding that the statement *"the prayer of a righteous person is powerful and effective"* is based on the righteousness you received as God's gift, rather than your own attempts at being righteous. Reflect and discuss on what that gift of righteousness is and how God brought it about.

Chapter 7
The "D" Word

In Chapter 5, we discussed the importance of devotion. Remember the definitions? One of them was *"ardent, often selfless affection and dedication, as to a person or principle."* [1]. We discovered that we are devoted to something we strongly believe or delight in and consider it worth investing our time and effort above other things in our lives.

Devotion starts with the letter "D." It involves another "D" word: *discipline.* Athletes know it well. But it seems to be a concept that is either hardly familiar or hardly popular in today's consumer-driven Christian culture. Discipline implies hard work and self-control, not to mention considerable time. One of the reasons why discipline is not a popular word in the Christian experience is because we already live fast-paced lives that require a lot of effort. Many of us go to bed tired, wake up just as tired, and simply don't feel we have the margin to add more to our already overflowing plates. But as we know from prioritizing activities in our lives, we set our minds on doing whatever we deem necessary, whether we feel tired or not. And that requires discipline.

The American Heritage Dictionary of the English Language defines discipline as "training that corrects, molds, or perfects the mental faculties or moral character." [2]. Discipline is not just rigorous physical training. It is first and foremost mental training. Both soldiers and athletes know this. According to George Washington, first President of the United States, *"Nothing can be more hurtful to the service, than the neglect of discipline; for that discipline, more than numbers, gives one army the superiority over another."* [3]. Legendary American football coach Vince Lombardi had this to say about discipline: *"The price of success* is hard work, dedication to the job at hand, and the determination that whether we win or lose, we have applied the best of ourselves to the task at hand." [4]

The Apostle Paul compared spiritual discipline to both:

"Share in suffering as a good soldier of Christ Jesus. No soldier gets entangled in civilian pursuits, since his aim is to please the one who enlisted him." (2 Timothy 2:3,4)

"Do you not know that in a race all the runners run, but only one receives the prize? So run that you may obtain it. Every athlete exercises self-control in all things. They do it to receive a perishable wreath, but we an imperishable. So I do not run aimlessly; I do not box as one beating the air. But I discipline my body and keep it under control, lest after preaching to others I myself should be disqualified." (1 Corinthians 9:24-27)

You get the picture: Dedication, determination, hard work, self-denial, self-control, suffering—none of it pleasurable, convenient, or entertaining. We could have seen that one coming. After all, Jesus talked about counting the cost of following Him and the road to eternal life being narrow. It begs the question: Why is discipline necessary, and what does that have to do with prayer?

Three Keys to Spiritual Discipline

You can read between the lines of these quotes and Bible verses that there are three keys to discipline: conviction, motivation, and a goal. That goes for sports discipline, military discipline, and spiritual discipline.

Discipline is rooted in the conviction that there is something worth striving for. Setting aside any deterrent and distraction, you are willing to do anything to achieve it, no matter the cost. In the military, it could be the defeat of an opposing army or the successful defense of one's country. Soldiers are willing to give up sleep, wear a uniform, train hard, and lay down their lives for it. In sports, it is the glory of winning first place and the trophy that it yields. Athletes train long hours every day, sometimes for years, pushing their bodies to their limits to win a particular tournament. In our spiritual life, we fight off whatever hinders us that we may find our sole delight in Christ, to be found a "good and faithful servant" and enter eternity in His presence.

The ultimate example of such conviction is Christ, *"Who for the joy that was set before him endured the cross, despising the shame, and is seated at the right hand of the throne of God."* (Hebrews 12:2).

The joy of bringing about the salvation of mankind and His exaltation to the right hand of the Father, where He was given the name above all names (Philippians 2:9), were His motivation to endure the agony and humiliation of being executed like a common criminal on a Roman cross.

Discipline also requires motivation. Simply having a conviction that something is worth striving for is not enough. Motivation keeps you going. It reminds you to take your eyes off the unpleasantness of exertion when you feel the pain and remember the joy of reaching the goal. Motivation produces perseverance, and without that, you won't finish the race. Motivation tells you to look ahead toward your goal, to keep pushing yourself, and not look back to the familiar of what once was. Take Moses and the twelve tribes wandering around the desert, for instance. They murmured, grumbled, got angry at God and Moses, tried worshipping another god, even wanted to go back to slavery in Egypt. Ultimately, sticking to the goal of reaching the Promised Land got them through it all. When Joshua took over from Moses and led the people across the river Jordan, he said:

"Remember the word that Moses the servant of the Lord commanded you saying, 'The Lord your God is providing you a place of rest and will give you this land." (Joshua 1:13)

Both *conviction* and *motivation* fall short if you do not have a *goal*. For the people of Israel, it was the Promised Land. For Jesus, it was the salvation of mankind and His return to the right hand of the Father. For the Apostle Paul, it was finishing the race and receiving the crown of righteousness (see 2 Timothy 4:8).

And for us? What is the goal of our spiritual discipline? When you read the entire chapter of Hebrews 12, you discover that disciplining yourself, as well as receiving discipline from the Lord, is worth it. The reward? In the end, we receive an unshakeable kingdom (Hebrews 12:28) and the face-to-face presence of God the Righteous Judge and Jesus the Mediator of our New Covenant. We receive the prize for having persevered to the end, having died in Christ, being saved from the wrath of God against rebellious humanity, and being ushered in the eternal light and love of His presence.

All that starkly contrasts the notion that discipline is a mindless routine you force yourself to do while your heart is not in it. Some other religions may have that as part of their system, but for a Christian, it always comes back to wholehearted love for God expressed in the uncomfortable, often painful exercise of discipline.

By the way, the word *discipline* comes from the word *disciple*. The Greek word is mathētēs, which means student. Jesus made it clear that He expected His students to renounce their possessions and their worldly attachments and focus entirely on His presence so He could teach them, coach them and mold them. Discipleship means the same for us: saying no to worldly pleasures and pouring our time and effort into our relationship with Him so that He can teach us, guide us, comfort us and change us. That is why Jesus said that following Him involved counting the cost of setting aside all worldly pleasures that distract and hinder us from growing closer to Him.

Prayer Without Ceasing Calls for Discipline

This brings us to the reason why discipline is essential for a vibrant prayer life. We already saw in Chapter 5 that unceasing prayer is rooted in regular extended times alone with God and in purposely fighting off distractions to make the most of idle moments throughout your day. That requires discipline, driven by the delight of being in God's presence, and by the duty of making that our top priority. The discipline part comes into focus when all kinds of distractions assault our minds, and our feelings tell us that being alone with God, meditating on the Word, and praying throughout the day are not as much fun as, well, everything else in life.

Trust me, I know. One of the characteristics of ADHD is to be constantly distracted by visually appealing things. Loads of words in black ink on page after page are not appealing. It requires a conscious and constant effort to do what feels counter-intuitive, namely closing my eyes and focusing my thoughts on the unseen God, and meditating on printed words I just read. It requires an equal amount of conscious effort to put my phone away and set my thoughts on God's Kingdom. I have to be thoroughly convinced that those things are worth it. I learned by trial and error that they are. I have also seen the damage that neglecting regular times of prayer does to my sense of God's presence and to seeing Him at work in my life. I have felt the weight of guilt and regret of neglecting to give my Creator, Father, Savior, Counselor, Provider, Sustainer, Protector, and Comforter who graciously pours Himself into me every second, every hour, and every day my full attention and effort. Those negative reinforcers help in the struggle to set aside the distractions I am naturally drawn to.

On the other hand, I have seen the rich rewards of devoting my time to the Lord. My journal contains page after page of glorious insights in passages of Scripture, God's miraculous answers to prayers, the sense of His immediate presence I experienced. They serve as my positive reinforcement. The memory of those delights awakens a hunger for new ones that are stronger than the appeal of superficial distractions.

In light of all this, we must embrace the D-word in our spiritual life, not shun it. God, first of all, deserves it. Not just that, He expects it, He delights in it, He rewards it, and He grows through it. Discipline is the key to holding on to Christ so we can bear spiritual fruit, love more, know God more, rejoice more, grow in faith, and be steadfast in all our ways. And it is a key to constant powerful and effective prayer.

Two disciplines, in particular, contribute significantly to a dynamic prayer life.

Fasting

Throughout Scripture, we come across examples of fasting as a religious practice among both Jews and Christians. Moses, for instance, fasted for forty days and forty nights on Mount Sinai while waiting to receive the tablets of the law (Deuteronomy 9:9). Ezra fasted for what appears to be three days as he mourned for the sins of his people upon his return to Jerusalem (Ezra 10:6). Daniel fasted and prayed for three weeks that he might understand the vision God gave him about a great conflict (Daniel 10:2-3). In the New Testament, Jesus began his ministry with a forty-day fast in the desert where the Spirit led him to prepare for an attack by the devil (Matthew 4:1,2). The Apostle Paul fasted for three days after his dramatic conversion on the road to Damascus (Acts 9:9). The elders of the church in Antioch fasted before receiving word from the Holy Spirit to send out Paul and Barnabas as missionaries (Acts 13:2,3). And Jesus referred to fasting several times in His teaching (see Matthew 6:16, Mark 9:29). By all accounts, fasting was a regular and standard practice among the people of God.

There is a close relationship between fasting and prayer, if not mentioned, then implied in all those examples. The general idea is that fasting is a God-ordained way of enhancing our prayers (see Leviticus 23:27). But why? And how?

First, fasting *emphasizes the need for us to hunger for God more than we do for food*. It is a short, intensified experience of Jesus' exhortation that man cannot live by bread alone (Matthew 4:4) and that we should seek the kingdom of God before worrying about material needs (Matthew 6:31-33). The physical hunger pangs you feel at the onset of your fast act as prods that our hunger pangs for the presence of God should be even stronger.

Secondly, fasting *deepens humility*. Such was the case with Ezra as he surveyed the temple's ruins that had been destroyed to punish his forefathers' sins. And with David, who afflicted himself with fasting when his prayers for deliverance from his foes went unanswered (Psalm 35:13). Fasting can make a person hungry and physically weak, even Jesus (see Matthew 4:2). That sense of human frailty makes our need for God acute.

Thirdly, fasting *intensifies our concentration while praying*. It helps us triumph over our senses. And it has a way of uncluttering the mind, which sharpens our focus. Sugar and carbs can create "brain fog" and negatively impact the clarity of our thinking. A fast helps clear that fog as our body burns off the sugar and carbs in our food. A clearer mind, in turn, helps us focus on God.

Fourthly, fasting *deepens our devotion to God*. According to Andrew Murray, *"Prayer is reaching out after the unseen; fasting is letting go of all that is seen and temporal. Fasting helps express, deepen, confirm the resolution that we are ready to sacrifice anything, even ourselves to attain what we seek for the kingdom of God."* [5] We don't have to prove anything to God. It is, first and foremost, an affliction we put on ourselves as a reminder that we are willing to forego our physical needs and sense of self-preservation for the sake of the kingdom. An athlete will say, *"no pain, no gain."* We have to be willing to undergo discomfort to reap the benefits of our discipline.

Fifthly, fasting *strengthens our faith*. When Satan confronted Jesus after His forty-day fast, He met him head-on from a place of spiritual strength, even though He was feeling physically weak. The replacement of our focus on food with a focus on God heightens our awareness of His presence, and that strengthens our confidence that He will see us through any challenge that lies ahead. Perhaps that is a specific situation for which we are fasting or a general sense of assurance and peace that comes from being near Him and having heard His voice more loudly and clearly than ever due to our heightened focus.

Last but not least: fasting *puts us in a better place to hear from God*. It has sharpened our spiritual senses, we are not thinking about food, and we are rising above the distraction of our natural senses. We are now attuned enough to hear from God. Perhaps that is why Moses had to fast and wait for forty days before God would speak to him. I think he came up the mountain with a head full of distractions. Obviously not the electronic kind we carry with us all the time. But leading the obstinate people of Israel through the desert must have felt like herding cats and kept his mind spinning. Perhaps he was ready with a list of questions to fire at God once He showed up. All of that busyness had to clear out of his head before he could receive what he needed to hear from God. I can relate somewhat. There have been many times when I would get alone with God for an extended time of prayer, and I could not concentrate. My mind kept wandering off to imaginary conversations with people that weren't there and who I was mad at, to-do lists, daydreams, and other forms of "stinking thinking." When I fast, pushing through hunger pangs helps me focus on God and ignore the million other places my mind wants to go. Then the still small voice of the Holy Spirit is clear and concise, and the impact of what He says cuts to my core. It is the difference between hearing with half an ear and listening intently. The more intently we hear, the more profound the impact of the

Holy Spirit says to us.

Fasting With The Right Motive

Just like praying with the right motive matters a great deal, fasting with the right motive does too. God notices. It matters so much to Him that He had His Son talk about it to the disciples since the religious leaders of His people had lost sight of it:

"And when you fast, do not look gloomy like the hypocrites, for they disfigure their faces that their fasting may be seen by others. Truly, I say to you, they have received their reward. But when you fast, anoint your head and wash your face, that your fasting may not be seen by others but by your Father who is in secret. And your Father who sees in secret will reward you." (Matthew 6:16-18)

The "seeing in secret" refers to what is going on in your heart, not in your outward appearance. God rewards a genuine hunger for Him, not a big show to impress others. He wants us to hide it so He alone can see it. When we are eager to do that, He knows our fasting is out of a genuine desire to draw near to Him. That is the real thing.

What also does not please God is when we fast out of religiosity, i.e., simply because our religion requires us to do it and not because we *want* to do it. To make fasting part of a religious set of rules means that you merely do it out of obedience to a command. Just like we can pray for the sake of praying as a habit, we can fast for the sake of fasting and not out of a desire to be close to God. Even though God gave the Jews a command to fast once a year on the Day of Atonement, which smells like following rules, it had a specific reason attached to it – namely to cleanse from sin. Take the specific reason out of it, and the fast becomes meaningless. By the time Jesus entered the world and began to clarify how the kingdom of God was supposed to work, fasting had become a twice-a-week religious practice for many of the religious leaders to prove that they were more spiritual than others.

Under the New Covenant, fasting is neither commanded nor forbidden. Jesus is more concerned with how you fast than whether or not you fast. If fasting seems repulsive to you, He'd rather you didn't. Religious habits do not impress God. Earnest, hungry hearts do.

Another way to get fasting wrong is to use it to try and force an answer to prayer out of God. Just like a child who all of a sudden starts doing the chores they never want to do in an attempt to impress their parents so they'll give them something they want. That kind of manipulation is a misuse of fasting because it does not conform to God's design for it. We are to humble ourselves, desire Him more deeply, focus on Him more strongly, listen to Him more closely. Fasting is meant to enhance our focus on Him, not on specific things we want from Him.

Then there is fad-fasting. I think it is probably a form of fasting to subtly impress others, but it is worth mentioning by itself. For instance, there was a resurgence of the 40-day fast a la Moses and Jesus in the early nineties. Booklets were written on how to do it, and people spurred each other on to do it, citing amazing stories of encounters with God. More recently, the "Daniel-fast" became popular. It is based on Daniel's partial fast I mentioned earlier and involves not eating meat or sweets and not drinking wine for a time. In and of itself, those fasts are not harmful, except that you may be tempted to do it out of a herd mentality or wanting to be able to experience and share similar stories rather than a genuine desire to draw closer to God.

Before You Start A Fast

There are two things to consider before you start a fast:

1. *A purpose* – whether or not you decide to do it as a regular habit for spiritual or physical health reasons, or both, a fast

is more meaningful if you do it for a specific reason. Perhaps you feel the Holy Spirit calling you to a fast. Maybe it is to humble yourself before the Lord or out of a desire to spend more quality time with Him. Have a reason, a goal. It will help you overcome the initial discomfort of a fast.

2. *Medical clearance* – it is wise to talk to a doctor before you start a fast, especially if it involves complete abstinence from food for a prolonged time. You may have medical issues that could make fasting bad for your health, and your doctor may advise you to consider alternative forms of fasting instead of abstaining from food.

Start Small

Since fasting involves denying yourself some sort of comfort or nutrition, which is why the Bible calls it "afflicting yourself" (Leviticus 16:29), you may want to start small – perhaps by skipping one meal a day, and work up from there.

If you would like to know more about the various levels and forms of fasting, you will find a more detailed guide in *Appendix A*.

Spiritual Preparation

One difficulty that folks have is to do a fast but struggle with engaging in extraordinary times of prayer and meditation on the Word. The most significant cause for that is a lack of preparation. You skip your meal, and you sit down for prayer, and then what?

It is essential to prepare spiritually for any type of fast. Perhaps you have a specific reason or purpose for your fast. Get a devotional or book to read that speaks into that. When your objective is just to draw close to the Lord and hear from Him, have a journal ready. Ask Him to lead you to a specific book or section of the Bible. You can go online and print out a commentary on that text for extra study. Perhaps there is a prayer guide to pray through or a devotional to follow. Maybe you can even list some things you want to focus on in your prayers. Then have it all ready and come with an open heart and an open mind.

The Discipline of Waiting

Waiting is not popular in our fast-paced world, especially here in the US. Progress has meant faster cars, faster airplanes, faster internet, faster phones, faster customer service (well.... sometimes). Our sinful nature craves instant gratification, so it feels counter-intuitive for us to wait. The advertising industry knows this. "Fast and easy" is being advertised as the value-added virtue of just about everything. We live at breakneck speed, an exciting life means being constantly on the go, and we seem to always be in a hurry to get to the next thing. I can relate. I only recently realized that I lived most of my life in a hurry and took little or no time to savor what each moment sought to give me - beautiful sights, smells, flavors, sounds, experiences. As soon as I had reached the thing I was eager to get to, I would "speed-savor" it and already crane my neck to look for what would be next. Introverted, more contemplative personalities are often better at slowing down and savoring the moment than extroverted doers and adventurers, but still – most of us *hate* waiting.

That is why I call waiting a *discipline*. It requires mental fortitude and self-control—a denial of instant gratification. A reining-in of our natural tendency to want to rush ahead.

Waiting is a spiritual discipline because it is part and parcel of intimacy with God. Abraham had to wait until he was an old man before God gave him his promised son. Moses had to wait forty days and forty nights on top of Mount Sinai before God even showed up to start giving Him the law. The Bible is replete with verses about waiting on God:

*"They who wait for the Lord shall renew their strength"
(Isaiah 40:31)*
*"Wait for the Lord; be strong and let your heart take courage;
wait for the Lord" (Psalm 27:14)*
*"For through the Spirit, by faith, we ourselves eagerly wait
for the hope of righteousness"* (Galatians 5:5)

It appears from the Scriptures that there are three kinds of waiting:

1. *Waiting for the presence of God.* We've all experienced the anticipation of the arrival of a friend or family member we haven't seen in a long time. *"Absence makes the heart grow fonder,"* we say. Once the wait is over and we are in their presence, the quality of our time with them is all the more precious. A friend who works for an amusement park told us that they employ the same principle. They purposely manage the wait time for the rides. When the lines get short, they shut down a few rides, so they get longer again. The idea is that the longer people have to wait, the greater their anticipation becomes, and the greater their anticipation, the more they enjoy the ride.

2. *Waiting for an answer to prayer.* God answers our prayers as soon as we say them. But the answers do not always come right away. Sometimes God wants to test the patience of our faith and bring us to the point where we cease our striving (see Psalm 37:7). At other times, we have to go through a period of preparation to receive the answer (see Habakkuk 1:2, 5). And at times, there is a spiritual battle over the answer (see Daniel 10:13).

113

3. *Waiting for the return of Christ.* The apostles frequently urged the believers to be patient, endure suffering, and look to the Savior's return with eagerness. (see Hebrews 9:28, Romans 8:23-25, Titus 2:13). In this case, waiting is a continuous mindset that influences our priorities and actions as believers.

The good news is that waiting on God is never a waste of time. When the people of Israel had to wait for God to dam in the river Jordan so that the water level would go down far enough for them to cross, they were instructed to use the time to consecrate and prepare themselves. Jesus taught us that we should always have an attitude of readiness and alertness while waiting:

"Stay dressed for action and keep your lamps burning, and be like men who are waiting for their master to come home from the wedding feast, so that they may open the door to him at once when he comes and knocks." (Luke 12:35-40).

Right in line with that teaching, He commanded His disciples just before He ascended into heaven to wait in Jerusalem for the promised baptism with the Holy Spirit (Acts 1:4,5). Nothing happened for seven days, but they used the time to pray and choose a replacement for Judas.

Waiting on the Lord involves alertness, readiness, prayerfulness, and faith that waiting does not mean "no," or "time's a-wasting, let's help the Lord out." Faith during waiting keeps our eyes firmly on Him, like a servant on his master, ready to jump into action the moment he gives the signal (Psalm 123:2). That faith stays active through persistent prayer, making use of the invitation that the Lord gave us in Luke 18:1, illustrating it with the story of a persistent widow:

"Then Jesus told his disciples a parable to show them that they should always pray and not give up." (Luke 18:1 NIV).

The reward of waiting is rich:

"The LORD is good to those who wait for him, to the soul who seeks him." (Lamentations 3:25)

"But they who wait for the LORD shall renew their strength; they shall mount up with wings like eagles; they shall run and not be weary; they shall walk and not faint." (Isaiah 40:31)

The reward is knowing and savoring God's presence, His promises, His fullness, in ways that we will never know when we hurry on.

Fasting and waiting are often related. While we deny ourselves food or other creature comforts and direct our hunger towards God, we wind up waiting for Him. Because we are unaccustomed to waiting, it may seem the wait is long, even though it isn't anywhere near forty days and forty nights. But the reward is not only a deeper experience of God's presence. It is greater faith and a stronger and more steadfast character. The saying goes that the most dangerous prayer to pray is *"Lord, teach me patience."* That is true, but only from the standpoint that it will involve a bare-knuckle fight with our natural tendency to keep pace with the world and hurry onward. In every other way, it is the best prayer we can pray if we truly want to savor God in each moment and thus deepen our joy and faith in Him.

Prayer Practice

How about it? Ready to try a fast and use the time to focus on the Lord and wait for His presence? Here are some suggestions to follow:

1. *Block out a designated time on your calendar.* Maybe one meal, perhaps a day, perhaps a whole weekend. Do what you feel drawn to, but don't overreach. Remember to start small.

2. *Plan your time.* Make sure you have a place to be alone and away from distractions. Perhaps it can be at your home. Maybe it has to be a quiet place on a lake, in the woods, or a friend's cabin.

3. *Decide what you are going to fast from and for how long.* If it is food, make sure you have plenty to drink. If it is electronics, make sure you can unplug them for a day or turn them off.

4. *Prepare your spiritual food.* Select a Bible passage or chapter, have a journal handy. Bring a devotional or a book on a particular spiritual topic you want to focus on if you feel so inclined.

5. *Be prepared to fight distraction* – hunger pangs, a craving to look at your phone, racing thoughts. One way to overcome it is to pray or read Scripture aloud (or in a whisper). Even the most veteran prayer warriors have said that it can take significant time and effort to rid your mind of all the distractions. Do not give up. It is worth it.

6. *Write down all the insights you received and anything you feel the Lord tells you to do afterward* – maybe to phone a friend, pray along certain lines, read a particular book, change certain habits or behaviors. Obey what He is telling you. Writing them down is important because we are quick to forget once we come down from the mountaintop and into the distractions of the world down below.

Questions For Reflection And Discussion

1. Jesus' definition of discipline involved counting the cost of following Him wholeheartedly. Looking back on your decision to surrender your life to Him, can you say that you counted the cost? What kinds of "costs" of following Christ along the way have surprised you?

2. List and share some of the highlights of your walk with Christ that have made the cost of discipline and sacrifice worth it.

3. If you were to add fasting to your spiritual disciplines, which type of fasting appeals to you the most, and why?

Chapter 8
With One Voice

During our ministry trips to Kenya, my wife and I had the privilege of staying at a training center for pastors outside Nairobi. The accommodations consisted of permanent safari tents mounted on wooden platforms, complete with queen-sized beds and spacious bathrooms. During our first night there, we were suddenly jarred awake from fitful sleep by the sound of loud voices. Groggy from jet lag, I glanced at my watch. Four a.m. What in the world? Alarmed at the prospect of some emergency like a wild animal or an intruder in the camp, I peeked out the tent flap. The tent across from us was packed with ministry students.

Some were pacing. Some were on their knees, and others were standing with their arms around their shoulders. All with eyes closed. Their mostly baritone and bass voices mingled together in a part-spoken, part-sung, part-shouted chorus of Swahili, and I realized they were praying. It went on for at least an hour, and further sleep was out of the question. Later that morning, the training center director explained that the students had been having their "quiet time." I learned that, unlike in the US, where we take turns, group prayer in Kenya is simultaneous. Everyone prays out loud at the same time, making for an exuberant and noisy affair. Our ministry trips to Latin America in subsequent years gave us the same experience – everybody praying in a loud, and often very loud, voice at the same time. I had heard similar stories from visitors to South Korea and other places in the world. It appears that our neatly organized taking turns method in Western Europe and the US is more of an exception than a rule in the global church.

This experience reminded me of one of the first prayer

meetings recorded in the New Testament:

"When they were released, they went to their friends and reported what the chief priests and the elders had said to them. And when they heard it, they lifted their voices together to God and said, "Sovereign Lord, who made the heaven and the earth and the sea and everything in them, who through the mouth of our father David, your servant, said by the Holy Spirit,

'Why did the Gentiles rage, and the peoples plot in vain? The kings of the earth set themselves, and the rulers were gathered together, against the Lord and against his Anointed' for truly in this city there were gathered together against your holy servant Jesus, whom you anointed, both Herod and Pontius Pilate, along with the Gentiles and the peoples of Israel, to do whatever your hand and your plan had predestined to take place. And now, Lord, look upon their threats and grant to your servants to continue to speak your word with all boldness, while you stretch out your hand to heal, and signs and wonders are performed through the name of your holy servant Jesus." And when they had prayed, the place in which they were gathered together was shaken, and they were all filled with the Holy Spirit and continued to speak the word of God with boldness." (Acts 4:23-31).

The believers lifted their voices together, just like in Kenya, Korea, Honduras, Peru, and many other parts of the world. But no matter how you do it, taking turns or all together at once, there is unmistakable power in united prayer. In response to the believers' prayer in Acts, the whole room shook. There was a fresh outpouring of the Holy Spirit and an infusion of boldness to keep preaching despite the threats they faced.

The Power of United Prayer

Jesus' teaching on the new order of God's kingdom included powerful promises about agreement and unity in prayer:

"Again I say to you, if two of you agree on earth about

anything they ask, it will be done for them by my Father in heaven. For where two or three are gathered in my name, there am I among them." (Matthew 18:19-20).

Two verses, two promises. First, the promise of the Father's response in agreement on prayer. If at minimum two agree on anything they ask, it will be done for them by the Father. We have to be a bit careful here lest we think that this means carte blanche to ask for anything our heart desires, as long as we do it together. The overarching principle of praying according to His will and in keeping with His kingdom's purposes applies here too. The disciples knew that at this point since they had already received Jesus' teaching on how they should pray. So, "anything" should be anything in accordance with the will of God. The dynamic of unity is clear here: God responds with pleasure to His children who are asking in agreement for things related to His kingdom's advance and the increase of His glory.

According to author Wesley Duewel, God not only honors united prayer, but it also carries great spiritual benefits and power:

"There is unusual power in united prayer. God has planned for His people to join together in prayer, not only for Christian fellowship, spiritual nurture, and growth but also for accomplishing His divine purposes and reaching His chosen goals. In unity there is strength, a principle that is true in all of life, in the family and nation and among the people of God. The principle of Ecclesiastes 4:12 applies in spiritual and prayer warfare: 'Though one may be overpowered, two can defend themselves. A cord of three strands is not quickly broken.'" [1]

The second promise is that of Presence. Wherever two or three are gathered in Jesus' name, He shows up. We have to take this promise at face value. The showing up, or "being among them," refers to His Spirit. He is among us because He is in us. And when we pray together according to His will, the Spirit bolsters our prayers with His guidance and an infusion of faith. The result is that we take our eyes off ourselves, our differences, and our limitations and set them on God in unity of mind and spirit. And in doing so, we are an answer to Jesus' prayer in John 17:11:

"Holy Father, keep them in your name, which you have given me, that they may be one, even as we are one."

Out of the promise of the Father's response and Jesus' presence as we unite in prayer arises an important dynamic: The synergy of combined faith. J. Oswald Sanders writes: *"Both Scripture and experience unite to indicate that there is cumulative power in united praying. Faith is infectious, and infection spreads where numbers congregate. Unbelief, on the other hand, thrives more readily in isolation. A single stick can kindle a fire only with great difficulty. Was it not at a united prayer meeting that the power of Pentecost was unleashed?"* [2]

Synergy is a physics principle. According to *The American Heritage Dictionary*, it is "the interaction of two or more agents or forces so that their combined effect is greater than the sum of their individual effects." [3] For instance, one horse can pull about 1.5 times its body weight, which adds up to about 1800 pounds. Two horses together pull not twice but four times their body weight for a combined total of around 4,800 pounds! The Bible recognizes that principle. Deuteronomy 32:30 says:

"How could one have chased a thousand, and two have put ten thousand to flight unless their Rock had sold them, and the LORD had given them up?"

In other words, with the Promise and the Presence of God, two people united in faith-filled prayer have far more spiritual power than one. That is what brought about the shaking of the room and the fresh outpouring of the Holy Spirit when the believers in Acts 4 prayed together. When we join together to lift our voices to God as one, our faith unites and grows exponentially, making it possible for God to grant bigger answers and bring about greater victories than if we try to go at it alone.

Benefits of United Prayer

There are no downsides to united prayer, only benefits. I think it is because God greatly prizes the unity of believers. Jesus spent much of His agonized time alone with the Father in the Garden of Gethsemane praying for unity among the future believers (John 17). Psalm 133 reminds us that God commands His blessing towards those who dwell together in unity. The Apostles frequently exhort the new churches not to let any divisions exist among them, that disunity is of the flesh and not of the Spirit, and that we ought to love one another since the God of love indwells us (1 Corinthians 1:10; Galatians 5:19,20; 1 John 311-18).

United prayer fosters overall unity between believers. When we take our eyes off each other and stand shoulder to shoulder to seek God together, our differences tend to fade away. I have seen this time and again. In citywide prayer gatherings where thousands of believers from hundreds of different churches came together to call on God, such prayer gatherings birthed love, commonality, community, and the desire to work together to bless the city. Interpersonal connections made at such prayer gatherings often birthed new cooperative outreach and ministry initiatives. I have had the privilege of facilitating prayer retreats for pastors. They would often arrive as strangers, sometimes even competitors, and leave as brothers with plans to keep meeting together and join forces in reaching their city for Christ. Thus, united prayer fosters brotherhood between believers, which multiplies ministry empowered by the Spirit of Jesus, who loves and empowers such unity.

United prayer nurtures our faith. As Dr. Sanders observed: faith is contagious, while unbelief thrives in isolation. When you join with fellow believers agreeing and expressing their desire for the same thing, you come back from such gatherings with a stronger faith. That carries over into your personal prayer life as you believe God for other things. United prayer also nurtures the expression of your faith. After facilitating group gatherings in churches where praying together is an unfamiliar practice to say, people have come up to me to say that they overcame their shyness and prayed out loud for the first time in their lives. They would tell me that they now felt more liberated in expressing their faith through praying aloud together and were hungry for more!

United prayer triumphs over Satan. Like in the early days of the church, as described in Acts 4, Christians regularly face spiritual attacks. Especially when engaging in evangelism and missions, both of which Satan hates because it robs him of souls he wants to keep in bondage. As we face attacks of any kind, God hears His children as they stand together as one army and call upon Him as our general to turn the tide in the battle. Missionaries encounter this all the time as they seek to share the gospel in Satan's playground, where people worship other gods and spirits. During my final year at Bible College, I did a church-planting internship in the Philippines for three months. The missionary family I stayed with told me that their house was haunted when they first arrived. Windows and doors would open and slam shut by themselves. Chairs and dressers would move by themselves. The walls had "hot spots" – small areas that were immensely hot – that moved around in places where there was no wiring, which locals knew to be a sure sign of evil spirits. So they brought in fellow missionaries and had a prayer meeting to cleanse the house and cast out the evil presence. The haunting stopped, the peace returned, and they could begin their work. This warfare aspect of united prayer is also why the Apostle Paul frequently asks the believers in the churches he planted to pray with him for open doors, deliverance, and rapid spread of the gospel (see 2 Cor. 1:10,11; Philippians 1:19; Colossians 4:3, 2 Thessalonians 3:1). In recent times, we have seen movements of united prayer in crime-ridden cities like Hemet, California, and Kali, Columbia, transform those cities. As prayer multiplied and revival came, the evil fled.

The results were stunning: drastic drops in crime, corruption, and poverty and significant improvements in education, healthcare, and overall quality of life.

Obstacles to United Prayer

You would think that united prayer everywhere would be common practice, given the importance the Lord attaches to it and the spiritual benefit it reaps. But no. Uniting believers in prayer, especially in Western cultures where individuality and privacy are valued more than community, has its challenges. Here are the most significant obstacles I have seen to united prayer:

Sporadic personal prayer. Prayerlessness at home begets prayerlessness in church, which in turn breeds prayerlessness in the community. It's a domino effect. If you don't pray much at home or value the importance of unceasing prayer, you're most likely not going to run out and pray with others. That is why church prayer meetings often draw only a handful of people, even when the congregation is enormous. I have conducted prayer meetings for churches of 6,000 and up with only 20 or 30 people in attendance. And when uniting in prayer is not a common practice in a church, participation in community prayer gatherings where multiple churches come together for prayer will also be a hard sell. Unless there is a crisis or a move of the Holy Spirit. Then we see people join together in desperate prayer, with ranks swelling quickly and united prayer overflowing in spiritual revival, at least for a season.

Fear. You want me to sit in a circle and do what??? I have heard from quite a few that they feel very private about praying and are uncomfortable praying out loud with others. That fear is enough to keep them away from a prayer meeting. I remember being asked to lead a 15-minute mini-Concert of Prayer during a Sunday church service. Recognizing the varying comfort levels with sitting in circles and praying out loud during a Sunday service, I began by giving people the freedom to pray in just one sentence or only pray in silence if they were shy about praying in an audible voice. "Be bold and be brief" was the motto. Prayer topics were given, huddles formed, and soon you could hear the mumble of people taking turns praying. But as I looked around the room, I saw a sizable number of people dotted around the pews, sitting by themselves with their arms crossed, jaws tightened, eyes fixed on nothing, refusing to participate. Their tense body language had fear written all over it. Unfortunately, they missed out on an opportunity for growth. Several who had participated came up to me afterward with joy on their faces to thank me. They had overcome their fear, prayed out loud with others for the first time in their lives, and felt they had experienced a breakthrough.

Individualism. A pastor once made a profound observation during a prayer retreat. He believed that the main obstacle to pastors and churches in a given city coming together to pray and do outreach together was not so much competition but individualism. *"We all care too much about our own rice bowl,"* he said. He went on to explain that he felt convicted about the fact that for the most part, he had only cared about what was happening in his own congregation and on his own campus, not in the community as a whole – let alone in other churches. Many shared his sentiment. I have seen this often when taking stock of citywide prayer movements, and I still see this all too often when I try to gauge interest among pastors and leaders in coming together to pray for a city. Some churches are barely a block away from each other and have no contact with each other, and other churches have no relationship with or impact on their neighborhoods whatsoever. During a prayer walk through a neighborhood in a major US city, the pastor who led us pointed to a church surrounded by a high chainlink fence with barbed wire along the top. Not exactly a welcome mat for the community. Large churches with sprawling campuses that have a lot happening on any given day tend to be too busy to pay much attention to what is outside. Only a major crisis in their community will move them to step out of their campus and collaborate with other churches.

One refreshing exception to this came at the height of the prayer movement another major US city. One of the mega-church pastors came and presented himself to us with the desire to be personally involved. He said he felt convicted by the Lord that he should tithe his time to the city. Those were not just words. He showed up at every pastors' prayer gathering, mobilized his leadership and congregation to participate, and served on leadership teams.

Individualism is not limited to pastors and churches circling the wagons and staying within their campus limits. It is a common tendency in our Western culture. Where else do you have sprawling neighborhoods full of houses with attached garages you can drive into, filled with entertainment devices and ways to dissociate from your neighbors? This keeping-to-ourself mindset tends to focus for prayer primarily on ourselves and at most people and situations with which we feel a close affinity. As a result, we are reluctant to pray for community needs, missions, a city, or personal needs that are usually the theme of a church prayer meeting or community prayer gathering. Again, I have seen that either a significant crisis close to home or a deep sense of conviction from the Holy Spirit creates enough despair and concern for people to step out of their comfort zones and participate in united prayer. However, our natural tendency is to be preoccupied with our own lives and not feel we have enough margin to be concerned about others we don't know.

The sin of comparison. It is innate to our sinful nature to compare ourselves with others in hopes that we come out looking good in our own eyes. That tendency to compare can produce opposite results: pride and envy. We can become proud of ourselves when we appear to come out better than who we compare ourselves with, and envy if who we compare ourselves with comes out looking better than us. Believe it or not, that carries over into ministry more often than you might think. With a few notable and refreshing exceptions, it has been my experience that it is often challenging to get mega-churches involved in united prayer because of a pervasive attitude of superiority over smaller churches. Mega-church pastors often send the "prayer guy" on staff to pastors' gatherings instead of coming themselves or will only get involved if they can have top billing and some sort of say over how meetings are conducted. Their congregations will by and large not get involved unless the senior pastor himself is and actively encourages his flock to join in. On the opposite spectrum, small churches sometimes bow out because of anger toward the larger churches. I know this because pastors have talked about that anger. They can't muster the resources to have the kind of dynamic programs that megachurches can, and quite a few have seen half their already small congregations drift over to the megachurch down the street because of their dynamic music and programs. The divisions caused by pride, inadequacy, and envy run deep and can easily keep brothers and sisters in Christ from uniting in prayer. It is not until an external force like a crisis or the internal force of the Holy Spirit's conviction restores humility and forgiveness that united prayer can flourish.

Dissension. Galatians 5:20 lists dissensions, strife, and divisions as works of the flesh that are out of sync with keeping in step with the Holy Spirit. Dissension occurs when we only focus on our outward differences and lose sight of what we have in common. It lies at the root of racial segregation, strife over political affiliation, doctrinal and theological disagreements, arguments over the right way to worship, and the like. Dissension and strife cause deep divisions and schisms between believers that are hard to overcome. A striking example of such division is the Great Schism of 1054 that divided the then-known Christian

Church between Roman Catholicism (centered in Rome) and Eastern Orthodoxy (centered in Constantinople). There were many disagreements, but the straw that broke the camel's back was an argument over one word in the Nicene Creed [4]. Today the Christian Church is known more for its dissension and division than its unity. That focus on our differences also stands in the way of uniting in prayer. It takes an intentional decision by dissenting parties to set aside differences for the sake of the higher good of unity in the Spirit and embrace what we have in common: One body and one Spirit, one Lord, one faith, one baptism, one God and Father of all, who is over all and through all and in all (Ephesians 4:4-6). We will never achieve unity by trying to agree on theology, worship, politics, or outreach strategy. But when we unite in prayer, and the Spirit of unity touches us, those differences tend to fade into the background, paving the way for brotherhood and joint ministry.

Ways to Unite in Prayer

United prayer is not limited to weekly church meetings and regular community gatherings. There are several other ways to join with others in intercessory prayer. While you can't replace the contagious excitement of praying together in a group that is together in one place, joining with other Christians that are like-minded but physically separated can be just as effective and exciting. They also provide opportunities for ongoing united prayer – prevailing together for specific requests or issues requiring continuous coverage.

Prayer Groups. Smaller than church-wide prayer gatherings, small groups of believers will often form organically to pray for their church, pray for schools (like Moms in Prayer International), or rally around various ministries' prayer needs and causes. During the COVID-19 pandemic, when meeting in person was discouraged for prolonged periods, online prayer meetings sprang up using conference calls or online meeting services like Zoom. My wife's ministry, True Identity Ministries, began weekly virtual prayer meetings that played a vital role in the continuation of the ministry. I have heard of many others going online to pray for their churches and communities as they grappled with the challenges of continuing life and ministry as normally as possible while at the same time trying to stop the virus from spreading.

Prayer Chains. Almost every church has them. Some missionary and ministry organizations have them too. They provide an opportunity to unite in prayer over specific personal or ministry needs. A good prayer chain should include periodic updates and answers to prayer that fuel joy and faith. Do you know a missionary? Sign up for their prayer letter, and you will become part of their support circle praying for their ministry and family needs. True Identity Ministries has a prayer chain that uses group texts. On many occasions, urgent needs were shared, prayers were exchanged, and answers were celebrated. It's a great way to fuel your faith and avoid feeling isolated in prayer,

Prayer Networks. These are usually broader in scope than a more prayer chain, which tends to be more local. A Prayer Network may have a specific area of interest or type of need. They may cover an entire nation or even the whole globe. For instance, Voice of the Martyrs (VOM) has a global prayer network that prays explicitly for the needs of persecuted believers around the world. You can download an app for free that will provide you with a daily country-by-country prayer guide and sign up for email alerts of critical situations such as the arrest of pastors in restricted countries or attacks on church groups. An example of a more general global prayer network is Operation World. Like VOM, you can download an app with daily prayer guides packed with continent-by-continent and country-by-country information on missions, cultural and spiritual dynamics, obstacles to the spread of the gospel, ministries that are at work there, and more.

People in the US can try national networks like Intercessors for America. They will email you prayer guides each week that help you pray for government leaders, legislation in the making, national emergencies, and more.

The beauty of these networks is that you learn a lot about God's work all over the world. Praying for brothers and sisters on other continents and learning about mission work broadens your horizons, deepens your sense of belonging to God's global church, and increases your understanding of how vast and varied His work around the world really is.

Prayer Events. From time to time, Christians from all over the city may be called upon to join together in prayer. Such gatherings fall under the category of community prayer gatherings but are usually broader in scope. They are often the result of a stirring by the Holy Spirit in the hearts of leading pastors and ministry mobilizers to join together to seek God for the city. On a national level, there is the first Thursday in May, also known as the National Day of Prayer, during which you can join simulcasts with thousands of believers joining together in prayer for the nation, in addition to local prayer gatherings at city halls and state capitols. Also, there may be special prayer initiatives for nationwide spiritual awakening and revival, often held in prominent places like the Washington Mall and broadcast all over the country, so you can join in online if you can't attend in person.

Crisis-driven Prayer. Just like the believers of the first church in Jerusalem responded to a crisis (the Jewish leaders' threats) in prayer, so in our day, Christians come together to seek God when there is a major crisis. A major crisis jars us awake to our human limitations and the need for God to help us. After the 9/11 terrorist attacks on American soil, churches around the nation were full of people on their knees in prayer to God. When the COVID-19 pandemic began to spiral out of control, Christians began to band together in repentant prayer all over the world like never before, recognizing the spiritual significance of a pestilence and the responsibility on God's people to seek His face and repent. Such crisis-driven movements of united prayer tend to be short-lived, but they can have long-lasting effects. Not only do they often stir a more vibrant personal prayer life in participants, but they can also spawn ongoing networks and gatherings.

Prayer Walks. Praying on-site with insight is the rationale behind prayer walks. I recently had the privilege of joining together with several pastors and leaders in the Edgewood neighborhood in Atlanta, Dr. Martin Luther King's old stomping grounds. We circled the area to seek God for a spiritual awakening in the city. We prayed at the MLK monument for a non-violent solution to racial justice to supersede the erupting violence. I have led Marches for Jesus around St. Paul and Minneapolis and participated in prayer walks in Amsterdam's notorious Red Light District when I was a pastor there. Such things may be way out of your comfort zone, but there is a tremendous thrill about walking through an area, letting the sights and sounds around you give you spiritual clues for praying, and lifting what you see to God in Spirit-led united prayer. You can do something like that with a friend in your neighborhood or a group from church around an area of your city. As you pray on-site, ask for the Holy Spirit to give you insight. When you pray back what you see, you involve God directly in the life of your city or neighborhood, opening doors for the gospel and driving Satan and his demons from the area. This is especially important before a significant evangelistic effort. Through prayer walking, you enter the strong man's house to bind him, so he can be robbed of his spoils by the preaching of the gospel (see Mark 3:27).

Impromptu Prayer. When a situation arises, act on the spot. Grab your phone and pray with someone. Another way to call for immediate prayer is to email a few folks and ask them to unite with you in prayer, or to set up a private Facebook page.

Praying With Your Spouse. There is nothing more powerful in marriage than praying together. There are many ways to do that, and every couple has to discover together what fits them best. Some prefer a regular devotional time in the morning, others pray together before going to sleep. My wife and I often take extended time on a Saturday to pray or have a mini-prayer retreat somewhere in the mountains or by a lake. And we often pause to pray together when a need arises. Praying together adds a dimension of unity to a marriage and it is my firm belief that God invests great power in the united prayers of a husband and a wife.

There are cumulative power and blessing in united prayer. It breaks through our differences, grows our faith, multiplies our strength, and intensifies our enjoyment of God. Fear or discomfort should not hold us back. The benefits outweigh the cost. We must learn to incorporate this in our spiritual lives to effectively battle unbelief within us, divisions among us, and the works of darkness around us. Our Christian walk is a group exercise, not a solo flight.

Prayer Practice

I encourage you to start incorporating two forms of united prayer into your spiritual life:

1. *Join a small prayer group.* They are usually not hard to find through your church. If your church does not have one, how about starting one? All you need is two or three others. You can discuss what to focus on and how you are going to format your time. You can find lots of resources on how to start a prayer group online that will help you get going.

2. *Sign up for a Prayer Network.* You can join a national network like Intercessors for America (www.ifapray.org) or a global one like Operation World (www.operationworld.org). That way, you can pray privately at home for a few minutes every day, knowing that you are joining thousands worldwide praying along the same lines for the same thing. Apps like Voice of the Martyrs and Operation World even show how many people have indicated that they are praying.

If you stumble across obstacles in your heart or the organization of your time, ask the Lord to help you overcome them. He is on your side! He values united prayer and wants you to engage in it because it is the best expression of the unity He loves.

Questions For Reflection And Discussion

1. What would you consider as your greatest hindrance(s) against praying with others?

2. How would you personally benefit from praying with others?

3. Reflect on and discuss why praying with others is so powerful, and why God has attached so much value to it.

Chapter 9
We Are At War

For a born-again Christian, in whom the Holy Spirit lives, everything in life has a spiritual dimension. Becoming a Christian means leaving one kingdom – that of darkness – and entering another – that of light. Once you make that transition, you join the people who are the focal point of the cosmic battle between God and Satan. Unfortunately, many Christians don't realize that for them, life is war, especially in the West. We live in a culture that trusts in the material world - what we can see, hear, smell or touch. As a result, we struggle to believe that there is a spiritual reality behind it all. We know in theory that Satan and his demons exist and that angels doing battle with them are real, but for most of us, their presence is hidden, and so we don't think about it much.

However, by ignoring or minimizing the spiritual realm's reality, we miss the entire backdrop to our prayer life. We are like an audience watching a play without understanding because we don't notice the set. If we don't understand that for a Christian, life is war, we don't fully understand the purpose and power of prayer. We may have heard of the term "warfare prayer" as one of the types of prayer we engage in. Warfare prayer is actually a misnomer. *All* prayer is, to a degree, warfare prayer. But in our consumer-oriented church culture, we tend to treat prayer as room service to make us more comfortable, instead of a war-time communication device to receive orders from the general and request reinforcements in the battle. Paul David Tripp writes: *"In this way, prayer often amounts to shopping at the Trinitarian department store for things that you have told yourself you need with the hope that they will be free."* [1] Treating prayer like that amounts to asking for things with the wrong motive, which we discussed in Chapter 6. The result is that it malfunctions (see James 4:3). The kind of prayer the Scriptures tell us will be answered advances the Kingdom of God - His glory and His purposes. Every prayer request Paul makes, for instance, has to do with him being empowered and helped in preaching the gospel. And every prayer he prays for his churches is for their spiritual growth. One of the most poignant prayers recorded in the New Testament, in Acts 4:23-31, was in response to threats made against the preaching of the gospel and was for boldness and courage, not for protection.

More often than not, church members request prayer to end physical discomfort and alleviate pain. In and of themselves, those requests are not wrong. Philippians 4:6 invites us not to be anxious for anything but make our requests known to God. But the absence of prayers about lost souls, the advance of the gospel, or personal spiritual battles is symptomatic of what is foremost on our minds.

Similarly, talk of Satan and demons is often avoided because it spooks people. We like to be comfortable in our everyday lives and not feel that we are fighting invisible evil spiritual entities. And that is exactly where Satan wants us to be. Two of his most effective tricks have been to either convince us that he doesn't exist or to let us believe that he won't bother us. That is why the Apostle Paul tells us in 2 Corinthians 11:14 that Satan disguises himself as an angel of light. As long as he presents himself to us as harmless, we will pay him no heed, and he can do what he wants. Says Timothy Warner in his book Spiritual Warfare: *"How "resist" got changed to "ignore" in so many segments of the Church, I don't know. When it did, however, Satan and his forces gained a great strategic advantage."* [2]

He did indeed. If we paid closer attention to the divisions, strife, quarrels, lovelessness, false teachings, and immorality

138

among us as believers, we would instantly recognize those as the work of the devil, not the work of God. Satan works hard to divide and conquer us. In contrast, God is at work to unite us and conquer the world with the gospel of Jesus Christ. God does not force His agenda on us. He wants us to seek it and recognize and resist the work of the enemy.

Because we are ill-informed about Satan and his strategies, we also often fail to see the man-made world around us as being in bondage to him. But all over the globe, he is working through political, religious, cultural, and economic systems to prevent the gospel from spreading and to attack the church because it is its primary agent. When he can't silence the church through persecution by anti-Christian governments, he will do it through the spread of militant Christ-hating religious movements or immoral popular culture. When he can't do either, he will do it through wealth and materialism that blinds people to the fact that they need Christ.

We are at war, and we have no choice in that. Satan's doom is sure (see Revelation 20:7-10), but until his defeat is a reality, he has been allowed to wield power in the world (see 2 Thessalonians 2:9,10). He is even allowed to wage war against believers (Revelation 13:7). Jesus likens him to a thief that comes to kill and destroy (John 10:10). He fights fiercely against any attempt to rescue souls from his dominion and bring them over to the kingdom of God. The good news is that God has limited his power and uses his evil schemes for His glory, and our spiritual growth and victory in Christ.

So much for peaceful, easy feelings. Not to mention a problem-free life. Hakuna Matata doesn't work in Christendom. To be sure, we have been reconciled to God, forgiven, redeemed, adopted as His children, sealed, filled, and gifted with the Holy Spirit, made citizens of heaven, and given assurance of our salvation from the coming wrath. That does not mean we can sit back and relax for the rest of the ride. God wants us to wage war and overcome. When we give our lives to Christ, we sign up for both eternal hope and for battle.

That is less scary than it sounds. We fight an already defeated enemy. The God of the universe, above Whom there is none equal in power, strength, wisdom, knowledge, truth, light, and love, is on our side. He does not throw us into a battle so that we will lose.

Not just that, but God has given us as redeemed human beings a position of authority over the evil one. According to Ephesians 2:6, God has *"raised us up and seated us with Him in the heavenly places."* From that place of authority, we may exercise authority over the evil one as we encounter Him.

Knowing all this, what does spiritual battle look like in our everyday life? And what are we to do?

Be Vigilant And Know Your Enemy

The most significant strategic advantage in any battle is to know your enemy – to understand his tactics, anticipate his moves, see why he is fighting you. That holds true for military battles, but it also applies to the spiritual warfare we are engaged in. In 2 Corinthians 2:10 -11, Paul urges the Corinthians to forgive a wayward brother *"so that we would not be outwitted by Satan; for we are not ignorant of his designs."* He immediately recognized that his immoral acts could easily play into Satan's hand by causing division if they did not forgive and restore their wayward brother.

Throughout his letters, Paul shows a keen awareness that Satan's attacks on Christians are not haphazard guerilla warfare but a well-coordinated war of attrition that employs weaknesses in our minds and bodies. In Ephesians 6:11-12, He mentions that Satan has "schemes":

"Put on the whole armor of God, that you may be able to stand against the schemes of the devil. For we do not wrestle against

flesh and blood, but against the rulers, against the authorities, against the cosmic powers over this present darkness, against the spiritual forces of evil in the heavenly places."

Paul is not the only one who mentions spiritual warfare. Peter likens the devil to a roaring lion, seeking someone to devour (1 Peter 5:8). Lions don't just go chase prey without rhyme or reason. They sneak around and scope out a herd for vulnerable animals. Then they roar to panic the herd. As the animals flee, they separate, making it easier for the lion to single out a calf or a weak adult to catch and devour.

The upshot of the Apostles' exhortations to be vigilant is that the human world around is currently held captive by Satan, who operates out of a spiritual realm and uses that flesh and blood to attack the people of God any way he can. His purpose? To kill and destroy anyone who left his dominion for God's kingdom. To make that happen, he drives wedges between us as believers and between us and God, and he undermines our spiritual vitality to ensure we are ineffective in the battle against him. More about that later.

Vigilance implies battle-readiness. First of all, we have to make sure we are continuously in a place of prayer. Our God-given walkie-talkie needs to be close at hand all the time. Just like a soldier who forgets or loses his radio and can't call for help, we can become vulnerable. This is another reason why prayer without ceasing is so essential. It keeps that radio on and the batteries charged. When we only pray sporadically, we start to feel cut off from God, our awareness of Satan's attacks begins to fade, and our faith falters. God seems far away; we receive no guidance from above, and we can't call for backup. When we feel far away from God, it is much harder to get back into a place of prayer where we can do what it takes to resist the devil.

Secondly, we must make sure the Holy Spirit is ungrieved (Ephesians 4:30). If we are aware of unconfessed sin, we should be quick to confess it. If we have not forgiven someone, we must do so at once. We have to let go of all bitterness, anger, slander, and bad intentions. Those are the things that grieve the Holy Spirit and cause Him to withhold His help until we set things right. We must make a practice of doing that daily and not letting it pile up and hinder our prayers.

I was recently convicted of that. I like to pray while driving, yet traffic in a big city can severely test one's patience. The busier it gets on the road, the broader the range of, shall we say, driving styles one encounters. And so I would find myself interrupting my prayers to mumble words of frustration at drivers around me under my breath. While that sounds innocent, it really isn't. The rising anger at a driver who cuts me off or slow-pokes in front of me is nothing less than a burst of pride – a sense of self-importance that expects people to get out of my way. The Holy Spirit whispered one day that that grieved Him, and I instantly knew that it hindered my prayers. Going from being angry at drivers one moment to humbly praying the next simply doesn't work!

Put On The Armor of God

We generally understand the battles that missionaries and evangelists face. After all, they are on the frontlines working to spread the gospel and snatch souls away from idol worship, bondage to sin, and evil. But is Satan all that interested in li'l old me, a follower of Jesus just going about my daily business? The answer is *"Yes, every Christian is involved in spiritual warfare."* Throughout the New Testament, the exhortations about spiritual warfare are intended for all believers, not just clergy, evangelists, missionaries, and people with a calling to be prayer warriors.

What that daily struggle against "rulers, authorities, cosmic powers over this present darkness and spiritual forces of evil in the heavenly places" looks like in everyday life becomes evident from the armor of God we are told to put on. A flesh-and-blood-soldier's outfit and weaponry are determined by the terrain, the climate, and the type of enemy he faces. For instance, one of the main reasons the Nazis ultimately lost against the Red Army in World War II after they invaded the Soviet Union was that they were hopelessly ill-equipped to do battle in the harsh Russian winter. Their tanks wouldn't start, their guns jammed, and many of them froze to death because their clothing was too thin. The Soviet Army had thick parkas, gloves, and hats, guns that were designed for their climate, tanks that could run in sub-zero temps, and the use of skis and snowshoes. With that advantage, they obliterated their enemy once winter set in.

Similarly, the spiritual armor, or "armor of God," is designed to give us the upper hand in the warfare we face. It was fashioned by the all-knowing, all-wise God, who knows our enemy better than we do. So we know it's perfect. Not only that, but the various components give us insight into how Satan attacks us.

"Therefore take up the whole armor of God, that you may be able to withstand in the evil day, and having done all, to stand firm. Stand therefore, having fastened on the belt of truth, and having put on the breastplate of righteousness, and, as shoes for your feet, having put on the readiness given by the gospel of peace. In all circumstances take up the shield of faith, with which you can extinguish all the flaming darts of the evil one; and take the helmet of salvation, and the sword of the Spirit, which is the word of God, praying at all times in the Spirit, with all prayer and supplication. To that end, keep alert with all perseverance, making supplication for all the saints." (Eph. 6:13-18).

Verse 13 begins by telling us to take up the *whole* armor of God. No soldier can do battle when pieces of his armor or equipment are missing. That's why commanders have daily inspections. Likewise, we are to take up every component of the armor of God to take our stand against the devil's schemes. Spoiler alert: when you look at the six pieces of the armor of God, you quickly see that they make up a spiritual mindset designed to withstand the devil's attack on our thought life. Most of the spiritual warfare we face is a battle over our minds, and each component of our armor equips us against the ways he attacks us there. God's intention with us wearing it is that we stand firm in our faith with minds directed towards Him and not to the world. Since Satan is trying to attack us in some way every day, we must make sure we wear that armor all day, every day. Let's look at the six components of the mindset God works in us:

1. *Truth versus lies.* A Roman tunic was held together by its belt. In our spiritual armor, knowing the truths of God's Word and the gospel of Jesus Christ form the belt that holds the other components together. It guards us against believing and agreeing with Satan's lies. Those come at us through our culture, through what people say to us, and through his attempts to distort the Scriptures (see Matthew 4:6).

   How to put it on: Declare to yourself daily that Jesus is the Truth and that you stand in full agreement with His gospel and teaching.

2. *Righteousness versus condemnation.* A soldier's breastplate protected his heart and vital organs. The breastplate of righteousness guards the heart. In the New Testament, the heart was seen as the center of our emotions and intellectual life. It stood for our soul, and that is where Satan, who is also called the accuser of the brethren (Revelation 12:10 NKJV), aims his blame. Whenever we mess up somehow, he is there to condemn us for it and call our justification in Christ into question. The obvious answer to this is Romans 8:1: *"There is therefore now no condemnation for those who*

are in Christ Jesus." This breastplate is impenetrable because our righteousness is not dependent on our performance. It is given to us by God based on the finished work of Christ on the cross and can therefore never be tarnished.

How to put it on: Declare that you are righteous in Christ and that your righteousness is secure and untouchable because it is based on Christ's death and resurrection, not on your success or failure at living righteously.

3. *Readiness versus laziness.* A Roman soldier could not march or fight without his thick leather sandals. Without them, he'd be immobile and have to sit out the battle. With them on, he is ready to go at a moment's notice. Likewise, Christians who do nothing pose no threat to Satan and are easily conquered. Proverbs 16:27 says, *"Idle hands are the devil's workshop."* (TLB). In my native language, Dutch, we have a saying like it: *"Laziness is the devil's pillow."* You get the picture. When we are lazy and passive, we fall asleep spiritually. We become depressed and inert. As a result, our Christian service suffers, our obedience to God lags, and our spiritual growth gets stunted.

How to put it on: Present yourself to God every morning ready to serve and be on the lookout for ways to be a blessing and a conduit of the gospel to the people you encounter, in word and deed.

4. *Faith versus Satan's mind games.* Roman shields were made of thick leather doused in water, so that flaming arrows from an enemy would be immediately extinguished when they landed on them. The arrows would often rain down in droves,

but the shields were large and offered superior protection. I like to refer to the flaming arrows (darts) Satan throws at us as the four "d's:" Doubt, deception, discouragement, and distraction. He constantly sows *doubt* into our minds: doubt that our faith is strong enough, that God has heard our prayers, that Jesus loves us. The list is endless. Since he is the father of lies, he also *deceives* us. *Discouragement* is another fiery dart. And o, can it burn! He constantly tries to convince us that we are failing in our faith-walk and might as well give up or at least not try so hard. Perhaps the sneakiest dart is *distraction.* The temptation to sin, to put other interests before God, to get addicted to creature comforts are all part of his game. They all look so innocent and attractive—anything to get us away from intimacy with God.

How to take it up: Declare that you stand in faith against doubt, discouragement, distraction, and deception today. Ask the Holy Spirit to help you recognize the darts when they come and resolve to respond with Godward prayer and worship, which keeps your faith strong.

5. *Godward focus versus worldly focus.* The Roman helmet, complete with face and neck guards, was a crucial asset to a soldier. It protected his brain. One blow to the unprotected head, and he'd be dead. The helmet of salvation does something similar for a Christian. Our salvation is our entry point into God's kingdom, gives us hope for an eternal future with Christ, and protects us against the hopelessness of eternal death and separation from God. It is the reason we keep our minds set on God's kingdom rather than the world. The words of Colossians 3:2 come to mind: *"Set your minds on things that are above, not on things that*

are on earth." In other words, the best protection against depression, anxiety, hopelessness, and worldly thinking is to remember that we have been saved from those bonds and by keeping our focus on God. Paul also admonishes us in Philippians 2: 12, 13 to *"work out your salvation in fear and trembling, for it is God who works in you to will and to work for his good pleasure."* Working out our salvation means that we focus on living the life for which God has saved us while relying on Him to change our nature so that we want to, can, and know how to live according to His design.

How to put it on: Set your mind on God's presence the moment you wake up and remind yourself of your salvation throughout the day, giving thanks to God. Learn to use idle moments when your mind is prone to wander, to think about God.

6. *The Word versus ungodly arguments.* So far, all the armor components have been defensive, designed to protect the wearer. The only offensive piece is the sword. It can be wielded to strike an enemy or ward off his attack. The Roman sword was double-edged, had a sharp point, and was just under two feet long, making it ideal for close combat. The "sword of the Spirit, which is the word of God," is His absolute truth given to us. It is the logos, the Word that proceeds from God (Matthew 4:4), revealed in the Scriptures and illuminated to us by the Holy Spirit; it is the primary weapon that defeats every argument set up against the gospel and against our faith (see 2 Corinthians 10:4,5). Just like a Roman soldier had to practice using his sword, so he knew how to wield it in battle, a Christian needs to know the Word of God inside out. - to recognize and refute false teaching, defend the faith, defeat the arguments against the gospel

that the world holds to, as well as Satan's distortions of Scripture aimed at confusing us. "It is written" (see Matthew 4:4,7) is the best offensive and defense against Satan's lies.

How to take it up: Immerse yourself in the Word. Read it daily and memorize as much of it as you can. The more you engage with God's Word, the more prominent it becomes in your thinking, and the more readily available when needed to ward off an attack or to share the truth of the gospel with someone.

Attacks come to us in all kinds of ways, every day. A few are blatantly obvious, but most are sneaky and disguised as "flesh and blood" through what people say and do. They can come through critical, sarcastic, or discouraging words. They can be a direct attack on our thought life. I have had days when I wake up, and the devil seems to be standing next to my bed, pelting me with negative thoughts about everything from my marriage to my ministry. Sometimes the devil attacks us through an ill-timed sickness, though not all sickness and disease are spiritual attacks. Often they come through the sensuality, the deceptions, and the lies in advertising imagery that surrounds us and pelts us with messages aimed at distracting us from God, losing our appetite for spiritual things while whetting our appetite for sensual pleasures. Satan tries to divide families, and he attacks through mental health issues, addictions, and eating disorders. I have found that he will often use an existing physical or mental health issue and use it to his advantage. The list of ways he tries to get at us goes on.

I mentioned a way to put on each component of the armor of God against all these attacks. But let me share the way I put on the whole armor of God in through a prayer I pray every morning. I usually do this at the end of my devotions or while I get dressed to start my day. It goes something like this:

"Father in heaven, thank you that you have given us a perfect armor to stand against the schemes of the devil. Today I go out in your truth and refuse to agree with any falsehood. I go out in the righteousness you gave me that was purchased for me by the blood of Christ and refuse to give in to any accusation or condemnation. I go with the readiness to serve that comes from the gospel of peace and pray that you bless those I come in contact with through my words and actions. I stand in faith to counter any doubt, discouragement, deception, or distraction. I set my mind on you in accordance with my salvation and citizenship of your kingdom. I want you to be uppermost in my thoughts and feelings and not get drawn back down into worldly thinking, depression, hopelessness, or anxiety. And I go out with your Word, letting it dwell in me richly so that I can defeat any argument set against the gospel of Christ or my faith in Him as my Savior and Lord. In Jesus' name, Amen."

There is one final note about the armor of God. It is no accident that it was patterned after Roman armor, which protected the front but left the back of the soldier exposed. The Romans built their warfare on teamwork. Soldiers marched or stood in close formation to protect each other's back, making an impenetrable phalanx with their shields, swords, and breastplates. Paul may have had that in mind when he ends his discourse with verse 18:

"Praying at all times in the Spirit, with all prayer and supplication. To that end, keep alert with all perseverance, making supplication for all the saints."

Spiritual warfare is most potent when done together. For that reason, we must be honest with each other when we are under attack and not pretend everything is just fine. At the same time, we should make room in our prayer life for our brothers and sisters who face attacks.

The Power of Praise

Author and speaker Judson Cornwall said, *"Saints who would learn to do battle for the Lord should first learn how to praise, for God sends praise as the shock troops to drive the enemy back before the rest of the army is allowed to join the battle."* [3]

The words "praise" and "shock troops" seem like they don't belong in the same sentence. We know praise primarily as worship and exaltation of God. But a weapon of warfare? However, there are precedents for that idea in Scripture. The first one is the conquest of Jericho by the people of Israel under Joshua. The entire chapter of Joshua 6 is devoted to it, but worth noting are verses 16 and 17:

"And at the seventh time, when the priests had blown the trumpets Joshua said to the people, "Shout for the Lord has given you the city. And the city and all that is within it shall be devoted to the Lord for destruction."

We see a similar theme in Jehoshaphat's battle against the Moabites and the Ammonites who had come to attack him. He took counsel with the Lord, and the spirit of the Lord spoke to him through a prophet:

"Thus says the LORD to you, 'Do not be afraid and do not be dismayed at this great horde, for the battle is not yours but God's." (2 Chronicles 20:15).

He was further instructed to send Levites and other musicians ahead to praise God:

"And when he had taken counsel with the people, he appointed those who were to sing to the LORD and praise him in holy attire, as they went before the army, and say, "Give thanks to the LORD, for his steadfast love endures forever." And when they began to sing and praise, the LORD set an ambush against the men of Ammon, Moab, and Mount Seir, who had come against Judah, so that they were routed." (2 Chronicles 20:21,22.)

Shock troops without spears and swords. Only songs of

praise. There seems to be a spiritual principle at work here. A direct link exists between praise and our battle against entities that are out to attack us. The sentence in 2 Chronicles 20:15 forms that link: *"Do not be afraid because the battle is not yours but God's."* Praise reaffirms that powerful notion. It lifts our minds to God, brings to mind His greatness, turns the battle we face over to Him, intensifies our prayers, and builds our faith. As we praise God, the thing that is attacking us begins to and God is magnified instead. That nullifies Satan's attacks, which are primarily aimed at undermining our faith in God. Satan recoils at us glorifying God because it robs him of the glory he seeks for himself by attacking us and ruining our joy in God.

Many of his attacks also aim to destroy the unity we have in mind and spirit with each other as believers. As we lift our voices together in praise, we close ranks and magnify God together. Agreement in praise and exaltation deepens our unity.

Praise frees me from negative thinking, depression, doubt, and anxiety and sets me in a place of prayer where I can exercise my God-given authority over the devil and his demons. With praise of God's greatness on my lips and security in my heart of who I am in Christ, I can resist him and see him flee (James 4:7).

Much more can be said about spiritual warfare. But the main two things to keep in mind are:

1. Life for Christians means war against spiritual entities out to destroy us, often making use of the world of flesh and blood around us.

2. In Christ, we have absolute authority over Satan as he wages war against us. We exercise that authority by putting on the armor of God, along with unceasing prayer and power of praise.

Prayer Practice

1. Write down in your journal a list of every way you sense that Satan is attacking you and how it affects your thinking. Ask the Lord to show you when you are not sure.

2. Read the prayer I wrote at the end of the segment about the Armor of God: *"Father in heaven, thank you that you have given us a perfect armor to stand against the schemes of the devil. Today I go out in your truth and refuse to agree with any falsehood. I go out in the righteousness you gave me that was purchased for me by the blood of Christ and refuse to give in to any accusation or condemnation. I go with the readiness to serve that comes from the gospel of peace and pray that you bless those I come in contact with through my words and actions. I stand in faith to counter any doubt, discouragement, deception, or distraction. I set my mind on you in accordance with my salvation and citizenship of your kingdom. I want you to be uppermost in my thoughts and feelings and not get drawn back down into worldly thinking, depression, hopelessness, or anxiety. And I go out with your Word, letting it dwell in me richly so that I can defeat any argument set against the gospel of Christ or my faith in Him as my Savior and Lord. In Jesus' name, Amen."*

Re-write it in your own words and put it on your bathroom mirror or your dresser. Pray it out loud every morning as you get ready for your day.

3. Think of a few phrases in praise of God's greatness and say them every time you feel an attack of some sort: negative thoughts, an unexplained fit of anger, a nasty thing someone does to you, a near-miss in traffic, you name it.

Questions For Reflection And Discussion

1. Not every difficulty you face is spiritual attack. How can you know the difference? Reflect and discuss.

2. Do you have a particular area of weakness or vulnerability that makes you more susceptible to Satan's "flaming arrows?" If so, how can you ensure he doesn't get the best of you?

3. Talk through each element of the armor of God as a collection of mindsets that protects you against Satan's attacks every day. What would each of those mindsets (e.g. truth, righteousness, faith) look like for you as you go about your day?

Chapter 10
Our Prayers Matter

Perhaps by now you are wondering, what happens to all the prayers I sent to heaven? And not just mine, but the prayers of millions of believers uttered through the ages? Some of my prayers I saw answered. Others I didn't. Some were desperate pleas during need or battle, and others were just me pouring out my heart to the Father. Were they heard? Were they remembered? Do they get stored up somewhere?

A Prayer Altar In Heaven

There are two beautiful pictures in Revelation that offer us a glimpse into what happens to our prayers. The first one is in chapter 5, verse 8:

"And when he (the Lamb) had taken the scroll, the four living creatures and the twenty-four elders fell down before the Lamb, each holding a harp, and golden bowls of incense, which are the prayers of the saints."

Our prayers appear to be collected in golden bowls, held by twenty-four elders. Scholars are still debating who they are because the Bible does not explicitly tell us. Most agree that they are humans, not angels. It appears that their white garments and crowns, mentioned in Revelation 4:4, represent two qualities of people who have trusted Christ as Savior and Lord and, as a result, were born again by the Holy Spirit. The white garments represent the gift of righteousness purchased for us by the blood of Christ, and the crown represents the reign with Christ by those who finished the course of their life without wavering (see 2 Timothy 4:8). I think that these elders in their white robes and crowns who hold the bowls with the prayers of all the saints – that's you and me – signify the acceptance of those prayers based on the righteousness and authority given to us as a result of Christ's death and resurrection. Remember James 5: 16? *"The prayer of a righteous man has great power as it is working."* We are righteous in Christ. That is good news because if it were based on our success or failure at living life according to God's pleasure, we'd all be in trouble! I know I would be.

But what about our authority? Doesn't that sound a bit over-confident? Ephesians 2:6 tells us that God, being rich in mercy, *"raised us up with Him and seated us with Him in the heavenly places in Christ Jesus."* Those 24 elders are seated around the throne, a picture of the authority we have in Christ. The authority with which we pray is not our own. It is ours only through our identity as being in Christ and Christ being in us. His Name is attached to our prayers. Our prayers represent Him, His will, and His authority on earth.

That's breathtaking! And all the more reason to believe that prayer matters. But there is more! Because something happens to those prayers after their acceptance in heaven:

The second picture is about that, and we find it in Revelation 8: 1-5 *"When the Lamb opened the seventh seal, there was silence in heaven for about half an hour. Then I saw the seven angels who stand before God, and seven trumpets were given to them. And another angel came and stood at the altar with a golden censer, and he was given much incense to offer with the prayers of all the saints on the golden altar before the throne, and the smoke of the incense, with the prayers of the saints, rose before God from the hand of the angel. Then the angel took the censer and filled it with fire from the altar and threw it on the earth, and there were peals of thunder, rumblings, flashes of lightning, and an earthquake."*

After seeing that our prayers matter because of their acceptance into heaven, we now get to see their impact. It turns out that we have a prayer altar in heaven, and what happens there is almost too amazing to comprehend.

First, an angel comes, takes the prayers of all the saints, and mixes them with incense – a lot of incense – to offer them up to God. They literally go up in smoke. A holy, sweet-smelling smoke, rising to God as a delight for Him. The incense represents intercession. That symbolism goes as far back as Aaron's priesthood. God had instructed him to offer incense inside the Holy Place of the Tabernacle representing the prayers of the people of Israel (see Numbers 16:46-48).

Similarly, the prayer and incense mixture rising before God on the altar in heaven are all of our intercessory prayers. Prayers that were prayed according to God's will and for the advance of the Kingdom. Pleas for deliverance from persecution, requests for open doors for the gospel, prayers for God to be glorified through the healing of a sick person, or His intervention in our everyday troubles. In short, all the prayers that follow the divine design Jesus gave us and are prayed with faith and from a pure motive.

The same angel then takes that censer full of our prayers, fills it with fire and tosses it back to earth where it causes a tremendous ruckus: peals of thunder, rumblings, flashes of lightning, and an earthquake.

Bible scholars disagree on what those represent. Consistent with the imagery showing that prayer matters, I think that the ruckus is something like this: In answer to our prayers, accepted on the basis of our righteousness and reign in Christ and presented before God as a sweet aroma in which He delights, He works powerfully to intervene, deliver, avenge injustice, and advance His reign in the hearts and lives of people.

God's Choice Regarding Our Prayers

In short: God has ordained to work His might through the prayers of His people.

157

Small people. Puny prayers. Big, big God.

Make no mistake about it. God doesn't need our prayers. Jesus even said: *"The Father knows your needs before you ask Him"* (Matthew 6:8). No, He *chooses* our prayers so that we get to participate in His triumphs over evil (see 2 Corinthians 2:14). He works through the prayers of humans to overcome Satan's evil aimed at humans. That's why the Great Commission – our marching orders to take the gospel to the ends of the earth – was accompanied with authority over demons (see Matthew 28:18 and Mark 16:17). The spread of the gospel is accompanied by the power of prayer that overcomes evil in people's lives and sets them free.

The Bible is rife with examples of how God chooses to work powerfully through the prayers of His people. Remember Hezekiah's prayer in Isiah 37? We talked about it in Chapter 4 and highlighted this all-imported phrase *"because you have prayed to me concerning Sennacherib king of Assyria"* (Isaiah 37:21). What ensues is a word from the Lord concerning Sennacherib that ends with an ominous announcement: *"Therefore thus says the LORD concerning the king of Assyria: He shall not come into this city or shoot an arrow there or come before it with a shield or cast up a siege mound against it. By the way that he came, by the same he shall return, and he shall not come into this city, declares the LORD. For I will defend this city to save it, for my own sake and for the sake of my servant David."* (37:33-35)

The verse that follows relates how an angel of the Lord went out and struck 185,000 Assyrians in their camp, sending Sennacherib and what was left of his army running home. Prayer, acceptance, judgment, miraculous deliverance, glory. Great things will happen when you truly believe that prayer matters.

And then there is Jesus Himself, whose divine blueprint for prayer we explored in Chapter 2. As the Son of Man, He modeled prayer as it should be in any believer's life. His example is perhaps the best proof that prayer matters a great deal to God, and because it matters to Him, it should matter to us.

Says author Philip Yancey: *"Jesus clung to prayer as a lifeline, for it gave Him both the guidance and the energy to know and do the Father's will. To maintain belief in the "real world" from which He came, to nourish memory of eternal light, He had to work at it all night on occasion or rise before daybreak..... Although Jesus offered no metaphysical proofs of the effectiveness of prayer, the very fact that He did it establishes its worth."* [1]

Prayer matters because it is so much more than daily acts or rituals of worship, surrender, confession, supplication, and intercession. It connects us to the heavenly reality in which God lives. By Him choosing to work through our prayers, He lets us walk in that reality. He opens our eyes to its presence, helps us understand and receive the truths that come from it, which put even the most mundane things of our lives into a spiritual and eternal perspective. I think that is part of what it means to be "seated with Christ in the heavenly places" (Ephesians 2:6). Not only is it a place of authority, but it is also seeing things through the eyes of heaven as we encounter them here on earth. Prayer keeps us seated there. It keeps us connected to the Father, open to the guidance and help of the Holy Spirit, and in touch with the spiritual reality behind material things. Neglect it, and you lose much more than God acting on your behalf. You lose that vital connection to the spiritual realm and the freeing, life-giving, truth-filled perspective it gives you.

Make Prayer A Lifestyle

When you realize that prayer is a constant connection to God's realm, it becomes easier to see that we rob it of its power when we limit it to an occasional or as-needed activity. While walking on earth as one of us, Jesus modeled it as a way of life so we could follow His example.

An early spiritual mentor of mine once told me that prayer should be as natural as breathing in and breathing out. Breathing is vital for our survival, and we do it all the time - anywhere from 17,500 to 23,000 times a day. Yet we don't think about it. It's automatic. It isn't until our breathing is obstructed that we notice its vitality. We consciously suck and gasp for air and, overcome by a fear of imminent death, momentarily realize we can't survive without it. But the ongoing act of breathing in and out all day long is instinctive and goes for the most part unnoticed.

Looking back on my 40+ years of Christian living, I see a windy and often rocky path toward understanding the full meaning of prayer. It has been anything but a smooth ride and a steady growth curve. There were failures, dry spells, lessons I had to learn multiple times because I was too dense to understand them the first time. I experienced breakthroughs and growth spurts. Like many, I began by only praying when I needed or wanted something from God. My prayers bounced back and forth between trivia and trouble. As a resident of materially prosperous societies, I was only vaguely aware of the difference between need and want. At times I got frustrated with not getting from God what I thought I needed, even though, in hindsight, I didn't. There were times when I coasted through life, and I hardly prayed at all. But as I slowly but surely matured by the limitless grace and patience of God, He put wise mentors in my path to help me along. Little by little, I learned the value of surrender, listening to God, and approaching Him on His terms rather than mine. I began to understand and incorporate a more multi-dimensional approach to prayer, including worship, confession, intercession, and thanksgiving. My motives for prayer began to change too. I slowly transitioned from me-focused prayer to kingdom-focused prayer. But it wasn't until my late forties that prayer truly turned into daily communion with God driven by a desire for His presence that went beyond ministry partnership, asking for things, and interceding for others. As is often the case, what I knew in my head took a long time to travel the 18 inches down to my heart. I am still growing and always will be, of course, until I pass from this world into His glorious presence.

As I compare my prayer life today to what it used to be, I would say that it does feel a lot more like breathing. I used to be locked into repetitive daily patterns and would feel guilty about breaking them, but not anymore. My prayer life has become more free-flowing. Instead of a guilt or necessity-induced daily ritual, prayer flows throughout my waking hours. Most days, I wake up with an immediate desire to get into God's presence and hear from Him. He is the first One I talk to after I wake up and the last One before I go to sleep. And in between, I commune with Him as much as I can in various ways. I respond to what I see around me with thanksgiving or prayer. I listen and look for His revelation to me through the Word. Sometimes I am just silently aware of His presence, and there doesn't seem to be the need to say or ask for anything. Frequently the Holy Spirit stirs intercessory prayer in me- at times intense and war-like, at other times more conversational. On those days, I spend more time worshipping and listening. I have learned that those are necessary to recharge after days of intense intercession or ministry that leave you spiritually drained.

Moving from Praying to Living a Life of Prayer

Why am I sharing all this? Hindsight is always 20-20, they say, and in that hindsight, I have to say it took far too long for me to realize that God wants His children to live a life of prayer, rather than to employ prayer as a necessity or a ritual. Not only that, but a life of prayer continually connects us to Him and the heavenly reality behind our earthly life and keeps the channels of His fullness flowing into us wide open. It is what Jesus called "abiding in Christ" (John 15:4-7). Constant, uninterrupted connection to Him that keeps us wide open to everything He wants to pour into us.

There are many standouts to inspire us along the way. James Hudson Taylor, the founder of the China Inland Mission and the first to bring the gospel to China, lived a life of complete dependence on God for everything. So did George Mueller of Bristol, who founded orphanages for thousands of street children, all without ever asking for a single donation and solely relying on prayer. Loren Cunningham, founder of Youth With A Mission, was known for locking himself into a room and laying face down on the floor in prayer until He had an answer from God on major decisions they faced as a ministry. The late Bill Bright, founder of Campus Crusade for Christ (now renamed CRU), was in my small group during a National Prayer Summit I had the privilege to attend. Throughout our prayer times, He would speak tearfully about His love for Jesus as the only thing that mattered in His life. Gladys Aylward, missionary to China, ministered where no others dared to go. Elisabeth Elliott, went to live among the Aucas in Ecuador who had a few years prior killed her husband. Corrie Ten Boom survived a nazi concentration camp and became one of the most influential teachers on godly living in the world. All had a deep connection to God through prayer, which enabled them to leave comforts far behind and minister powerfully and fearlessly everywhere the Lord sent them.

These are but a few who learned to do everything by prayer. Biographies have been written about them. Frankly, I secretly resented them for being examples of prayer power and intimacy with God to which I could never attain, until I realized that they were people just like me - flawed, imperfect, and inconsistent at times. They struggled with depression and unbelief and experienced spiritual droughts and times of doubt. What set them apart? It was an unwavering commitment to surrender to God, live in complete dependence on Him, and make Him their first love. They sought Him for Who He is, rather than for what He could do for them. They did not just pray on occasion; their whole lives were prayer saturated.

Good news! The spiritual secret they discovered is available to all of us: when we seek only the hand of God, we miss His face. When we seek His face, we get both His face and His hand. Say what?? When we focus only on what God can do for us, we miss an ocean of beauty and delight that comes from getting to know Him. When we aim to seek His face, i.e., get to know Him for Who He is, we also receive His hand – His action on our behalf.

That is how we move from prayer as a more or less occasional activity to a life of prayer that keeps us in constant communion with the God we love. We must make it our aim to seek Him whether He gives us what we ask for or not. His desire is for us to get to know Him - His character, His attributes, His thoughts, His feelings, His pleasures, and displeasures. When that becomes our aim, praying becomes as natural as breathing and as free-flowing as the wind.

There is no formula to make this happen. Your journey will be different from mine, and mine was different from the people whose biographies I read. But our journeys have the same starting point: Realizing the need to seek the face of God, not knowing how to go about that, and asking God to fill us with an all-consuming desire to know Him and guide us in moving from praying to living a life of prayer.

Apart from desiring Him more than the world, the only two ingredients that are needed are time and effort on our part. According to Hebrews 11:6, He rewards those who earnestly seek Him. Similarly, James 4:8 promises that when we draw near to God, He draws near to us. The seeking, the drawing near, must come from us. We then find Him to be responsive. He rewards us with His presence, love, help, and strength, His transforming power, the infusion of His life into ours, His counsel, and protection.

One of the most encouraging truths in Scripture comes from Isaiah 62:3,4 –

"You shall be a crown of beauty in the hand of the Lord, and a royal diadem in the hand of God. You shall no more be termed Forsaken, and your land shall no more be termed Desolate, but you shall be called My Delight Is In Her, and your land Married, for the Lord delights in you."

We have received the gift of righteousness in Christ. We have been adorned with holiness and freedom from guilt. We are a new creation in Christ so that God can do what He created us for: delight in our awe for Him, expressed in surrendered, God-glorifying, kingdom-seeking, desire-driven, worship-soaked prayer. All we have to do is decide to make that our priority and the bedrock of our daily lives, and He will give us understanding, help us grow, overcome obstacles, and set us free from what hinders us.

A Fight Worth Fighting

Unfortunately, nothing like that happens without a fight. My journey from occasional prayer to a life of prayer was full of obstacles, detours, and confusion. Our sinful nature will fight us from within because a life of prayer runs contrary to human reasoning and carnal desires. Hence the confusion and doubts. And Satan will fight us from the outside because He fears the power of praying Christians. Hence the obstacles and detours. But it's a fight worth fighting because of the supreme worth of knowing God and receiving all the benefits of His grace He extends to us when we seek Him.

Moreover, pursuing prayer as a lifestyle is a matter of spiritual life or death. Once we enter the kingdom of God through repentance and regeneration, our life takes on qualities that Scripture describes as a pursuit, a race, and a fight. Paul urges Timothy in 1 Timothy 6:11,12:

"But as for you, O man of God, flee these things (love of money and its cravings – see verse 10). Pursue righteousness, godliness, faith, steadfastness, gentleness. Fight the good fight of the faith."

A couple of years later, just before his martyrdom in Rome, Paul writes to Timothy again and describes his own life in similar terms:

"I have fought the good fight, I have finished the race, I have kept the faith. Henceforth there is laid up for me the crown of righteousness, which the Lord, the righteous judge, will award to me on that day, and not only to me but also to all who have loved his appearing." (2 Timothy 4:7,8)

Not only did we sign up for duty in the cosmic battle between God and Satan when we surrendered our lives to Christ, but we also entered a race toward heaven and a fight for our faith. The race does not involve speed as much as it requires endurance and focus since the course is littered with challenges, distractions, and obstacles. To keep believing till the end is a fight because of everything Satan uses to try and drag us back to his dominion.

Prayer in all its facets is essential to finishing the race and fighting the good fight. Through prayer, you receive strength and direction in the battles we face. You receive counsel and insight in His Word. You receive truth and godly perspective on all the confusion and lies that come at you from the world. You receive comfort, peace, and joy. You receive spiritual power, uncontaminated love, courage, and boldness in ministry. Prayer is what connects you to Christ, just as a branch attaches itself to the Vine. And through that connection, you receive all the vitality you need to keep running, keep fighting and keep growing till the end. Hence, it is the most basic and foundational of the spiritual disciplines and the one that is attacked and neglected the most, since our flesh, the world, and Satan do all they can to keep you from praying, especially from embracing a lifestyle of prayer. That's why it is a fight worth fighting.

Prayer Practice

1. Express to God your desire to move from occasional prayer to a life of prayer and your need for His help to do so. If you don't have that desire, confess it and ask Him to ignite it in your heart. You'll have an instant experience of personal revival!

2. Read Revelation 4, 5:8, and 8:1-5. Ask the Lord to give you insight. Then, every day you seek God in prayer, re-read Revelation 8:1-5, and let the imagery of what happens to our prayers fuel your faith that prayers matter a great deal to God.

Questions For Reflection And Discussion

1. What is the difference between occasional prayer and a life of prayer?

2. Why is a life of prayer essential for a Christian?

3. God has chosen to make the prayers of His people a vital element of advancing His Kingdom and accomplishing His purposes in the world. What are some of the ways He works through your prayers?

Notes

Chapter 1

1. John Mark Comer – The Ruthless Elimination Of Hurry, Waterbrook 2009, page 27.
2. Larnelle Harris & Phil McHugh – I Miss My Time With You, © BMG Rights Management, Universal Music Publishing Group
3. Andrew Murray – Quotes on Prayer, taken from www.prayerquotes.com

Chapter 2

1. Helen Howarth Hemmel - The Heavenly Vision (Turn Your Eyes Upon Jesus) 1922, Public Domain.
2. https://www.lexico.com/definition/supplication
3. John Piper – Prayer, Pursuing Peoples When Life Is War And God Is Sovereign, www.desiringgod.org February 1, 2001
4. John Piper – Does God "Lead Us Into Temptation?", www.desiringgod.org March 30, 2009.

Chapter 3

1. Magnificat is Latin. It means "he, she, or it magnifies." Latin often leaves out the subject of a sentence, and so a more complete translation would be "My soul magnifies [the Lord]

Chapter 4

1. Oswald Chambers - My Utmost For His Highest, November 8, Discovery House Publishers 1992

Chapter 5

1. Victor Frankl - Man's Search For Meaning, Beacon Press 2006
2. E.M. Bounds - Purpose in Prayer page 36, Whitaker House 1997.
3. How Much Time of An Average Life is Spent Waiting? www. reference.com
4. Merriam Webster Dictionary – www.merriamwebster.com/ dictionary/devotion
5. The American Heritage Dictionary of the English Language, Fifth Edition, Dell 2012
6. Strong's Exhaustive Concordance #4342, Hendrickson Publishers 2009

Chapter 7

1. The American Heritage Dictionary of the English Language, Fifth Edition, Dell 2012
2. The American Heritage Dictionary of the English Language, Fifth Edition, Dell 2012
3. www.searchquotes.com/quotes/about/discipline/
4. www.searchquotes.com/quotes/about/discipline/
5. From:https://prayer-coach.com/prayer-quotes-andrew-murray/

Chapter 8

1. Wesley Duewel - Mighty Prevailing Prayer page 123, Francis Asbury Press 1990
2. J. Oswald Sanders - Prayer Power Unlimited Page 155, Moody Press 1988
3. The American Heritage Dictionary of the English Language, Fifth Edition, Dell 2012
4. Ligonier Ministries – The Great Schism of 1054 by Stephen Nichols

Chapter 9
1. Paul David Tripp – New Morning Mercies (April 2 reading), Crossway 2014
2. Timothy Warner - Spiritual Warfare page 79, Crossway Books 1991
3. Judson Cornwall - Let us Praise pg. 44-45, Read How You Want 2015

Chapter 10
1. Philip Yancey- Prayer, Does It Make A Difference page 80,81, Zondervan 2006

PRAYER MATTERS

Appendix A
Levels and Forms of Fasting

Intermittent Fasts

A good way to start the discipline of fasting is with an intermittent fast. Skip one meal and use the time that you usually take that meal for prayer. If you intend to do a complete fast over multiple days, you may want to slowly increase the number of meals you skip to let your body get used to the physical effects of being withheld the food it expects.

Use the mealtimes you skip for prayer. You'll feel hungry; your body screams at you to put food into it at first until it gets used to the withholding. Let those hunger pangs drive you to God by expressing a greater hunger for Him in prayer and worship than for food.

Partial Fasts

As an alternative to complete abstinence from food, you may want to consider a partial fast. The idea behind it is the same: abstinence from food-based comfort to focus on God. In case you are wondering, I don't think it makes you a less spiritual person if you only do a partial fast instead of a full fast. God is more interested in your heart during the fast than in the type of fast you engage in. There are several ways to do a partial fast:

a. *Fasting from snacks* – if you are an in-between-meals snack monster like me, cut those out for a day, or multiple days, to use your snack breaks for prayer.

b. *Fasting from caffeine* – perhaps you are caffeine dependent (Guilty. Again!). Cutting out caffeine is more of a process than cutting out snacks since your body will suffer caffeine withdrawal that may cause headaches and fatigue for a few days. It will require willpower to seek God despite your discomfort, and that is why a caffeine fast is worthwhile! After a few days, the craving will stop, and you can use your coffee breaks for prayer with greater ease.

c. *Juice fast* – Known perhaps more for its health benefits, a juice fast is another viable alternative to a solid food fast, as long as you use the shortened mealtime when you drink juice instead of eating solid food for prayer. I have met some folks who did a forty-day fast this way. Juice fasts give you a double whammy: it improves your physical health by detoxing your body and building your immune system as well as your spiritual health by enhancing your brainpower to give you clearer focus in prayer!

d. *Daniel Fast* – The Daniel fast has become a popular way of engaging people who are unfamiliar with fasting and might be nervous about trying it. It is more of a diet than an actual fast, but I have seen numerous congregations do it together around a common theme. Many do it for a specific period, like 14 or 21 days. It is different from all other fasts in that you only eat certain types of food – the same types Daniel ate while in the king's court. During his first fast (see Daniel 1:12), he only ate veggies and drank water. During his second fast (see Daniel 10:2,3), he abstained from wine, meat, and "delicacies." A Daniel fast can be as restrictive as only eating vegetables and drinking water and as loosey-goosey as cutting out meat, alcohol, and sweets while allowing things like grains, fruit, milk, coffee, and juice. You are still eating meals during this type of fast, so the idea behind it is to do it for a time as a way of reconsecrating yourself to God. In a way, you are saying to God, *"I want the pursuit of my physical health through this diet to spur me on to pursue spiritual health as well."* A good way of doing that is to set aside daily times of extended prayer for the duration of your Daniel fast.

Full Fasts

A full fast is when you abstain from any food for a day or multiple days. When you have worked your way up to it as described above, be sure to drink plenty of water throughout the day so that you don't get hydrated. This is called a *standard fast*. You can also take it a step further and do an *absolute fast*, during which you eat or drink nothing. That is the most stringent form of fasting. Moses took to it in Deuteronomy 9:18 because of the sin Israel committed by worshiping a Golden Calf during his encounter with God on Mount Sinai.

I have done standard fasts for one day and multiple days. During the first mealtime or two, I found that you want to think about food all the time, especially when you feel the hunger pangs. One way to get past that is to respond to every thought about food or every hunger pang with prayer and a swig or two of water. Soon you have trained your mind not to pay attention to your body's demands for food but redirect its focus to God. After a while, you pretty much stop craving food or thinking about it, freeing your mind for a more prolonged and clear focus on the things of God.

Non-food Fasts

Quite a few people have embraced other ways of fasting instead of food fasts. The principle is the same: deny yourself means of entertainment or pleasure that you would typically fill your spare time with and use that time for prayer instead.

Examples of non-food fasts that I have seen people engage in are: turning your smartphone off for one or more days, leaving the TV or the computer off (except perhaps for work), abstaining from video games, staying off social media, not going out for dinner on Friday nights, and leaving the car radio off. All as a way to use the time and attention spent on that to draw near to God.

Acknowledgements

There is no way that I could have written this book without daily answers to prayer. The Holy Spirit met me each time I sat at the keyboard and put trains of thought into my head far too brilliant for my own brain to conceive.

On the human level, I am deeply indebted to a handful of people whose help was invaluable for this book to reach its publishable form. First, my wife Jennifer, whose prayer, encouragement, and input propelled me forward towards completion. Chuck Etzweiler and Steve Loopstra gave of their time and insight to read the manuscript and provide valuable feedback and input. And then, there is our dear friend Erika Hill. She put her editorial background and experience to use to patiently dissect every paragraph and help me see ways to make it better. I am a better writer because of her. Last, but not least, a number of our friends interceded for me daily, and by their faithful prayers have helped me greatly.

About the Author

Remco Brommet is a pastor, spiritual growth teacher, and prayer leader with over 40 years' experience in Europe, Southeast Asia, Africa, and the US. Born and raised in the Netherlands and pastoring his first church in Amsterdam, he moved to the US in 1986, after meeting and marrying his wife, Jennifer, in Amsterdam. He and Jennifer currently live north of Atlanta, Georgia, USA.

When not writing books, he blogs at www.deeperlifeblog.com and assists his wife as content developer and prayer coordinator for *True Identity Ministries* (www.trueidentityministries.org). As a couple, Jennifer and Remco are passionate about bringing people into a deeper relationship with Christ.

Made in the USA
Middletown, DE
21 June 2022

67390324R00106